Pennsylvania
WINERIES

Pennsylvania WINERIES

LINDA JONES MᶜKEE
&
RICHARD CAREY

STACKPOLE
BOOKS

Cover: Chancellor grapes, almost ready to pick, at Nissley Vineyards in Bainbridge, Pennsylvania. Photo by Linda Jones McKee.

Copyright © 2000 by Stackpole Books

Published by
STACKPOLE BOOKS
5067 Ritter Road
Mechanicsburg, PA 17055
www.stackpolebooks.com

Printed in the United States of America

10 9 8 7 6 5 4 3 2 1

FIRST EDITION

Interior design by Beth Oberholtzer
Layout by Kerry Jean Handel
Interior photos by the authors
Cover design by Caroline Stover

The authors and the publisher encourage all readers to visit the wineries and sample their wines and recommend that those who consume alcoholic beverages travel with a nondrinking driver.

Library of Congress Cataloging-in-Publication Data

McKee, Linda Jones.
    Pennsylvania wineries / Linda Jones McKee and Richard Carey.—1st ed.
      p.   cm.
    Includes index.
    ISBN 0-8117-2877-3
    1. Wine and wine making—Pennsylvania. 2. Wineries—Pennsylvania—Guidebooks. 3. Pennsylvania—Guidebooks. I. Carey, Richard, 1944– II. Title.

TP557 .C365 2000
641.2′2′09748—dc21

                                                   99-043759

CONTENTS

❧ FOREWORD

PENNSYLVANIA'S WINE HISTORY DATES BACK MORE THAN THREE HUNDRED years and is colorful as well as lengthy. In 1683 William Penn planted his first vineyard in what is now Philadelphia's Fairmount Park. Just over a century later, in 1787, the first successful commercial vineyard in the United States was founded by Pierre Legaux along the banks of the Schuylkill River, 9 miles northwest of Philadelphia in Spring Mill. Shareholders in his Pennsylvania Vine Company included many prominent Americans of the day, among them Alexander Hamilton, Aaron Burr, Johns Hopkins, Robert Morris, and Citizen Genet.

Starting in 1807, the Harmonists, a religious sect that had been founded in Germany by George Rapp, planted vineyards in western Pennsylvania north of Pittsburgh. The arched stone cellars that could hold 30,000 gallons of wine can still be seen today at Old Economy Village. In 1900 all of Pennsylvania's sixty-seven counties were making wine, with a total production of 195,627 gallons.

The start of Prohibition in 1920 brought all commercial winemaking to a halt. When Prohibition ended in 1933, the Pennsylvania Liquor Control Board had been established, and strict laws governing the production and sale of wine in Pennsylvania were passed. Though wine could be made in the state, it could be sold only through the stores operated by the Pennsylvania Liquor Control Board.

Interest in growing wine grapes and making wine on a commercial scale was slow to rekindle after Prohibition, and it was not until the 1960s that several growers in Erie County began working together to have changes made in the law. As the result of their efforts, in 1968, the Limited Winery Act was passed, which permitted wineries to make up to

50,000 gallons of wine from Pennsylvania-grown grapes. Wineries could sell their wine at the winery to individuals and, as well, to hotels, restaurants, clubs, and the Pennsylvania Liquor Control Board.

The first two wineries in the state, Presque Isle Wine Cellars and Penn Shore Vineyards, were licensed in 1969 and opened their doors in 1970. During the next thirty years, nearly one hundred limited wineries came into existence. Fifty-three of these are currently open and are the focus of this tour guide. An additional seven are in the process of opening. If these wineries are counted, half of the wineries in the state will have opened since 1990. The modern wine industry in Pennsylvania is this new.

Grape growing and winemaking require capital and a great deal of hard work, and the men and women responsible for building the industry dedicated themselves to the task. Although they came from different backgrounds, they shared in common a determination to succeed. As a group, they are among the most completely alive people I know, and it is a feeling that both authors must share.

The best tour guides are those that go beyond a simple recital of facts and pleasant accompanying photographs. Linda Jones McKee and Richard Carey have captured the personality of each winery and the people involved. This is no small achievement and was made possible in part by the different perspectives contributed by each author. Linda Jones McKee has been my business partner in L&H Photojournalism since 1981. She first became acquainted with the Pennsylvania wine industry through the pages of *The Pennsylvania Grape Letter and Wine News*. Working together, we established the magazine *Wine East* in May 1981. Her nearly twenty years of familiarity with Pennsylvania grapes and wine shows on every page. Richard Carey is both a wine consultant and president of Vitis Research, Inc., an electronic publishing firm in Lancaster, Pennsylvania. He came to Pennsylvania from California, where he had his own winery and experience in teaching enology at the California State University in Fresno as well as other educational institutions. As a relative newcomer to Pennsylvania, but not to wine, his insights provide another vantage point from which to view the industry.

As the authors well know, visiting wineries can be fun as well as educational, and they have presented anecdotal material along with practical information such as wine lists, hours open, and how to get to each winery. Through the profiles of the wineries, readers may very well anticipate what a visit to a particular winery will be like. They may also become fascinated by the vibrant Pennsylvania wine industry, an outcome that the authors would think made their efforts worthwhile.

Hudson Cattell
Lancaster, Pennsylvania

INTRODUCTION

WHEN WE DECIDED TO WRITE THIS GUIDE TO PENNSYLVANIA WINERIES, we quickly came to the conclusion that the only way to approach it was to visit every winery in the state, all fifty-three of them. That number isn't impossible, but the wineries are spread from Philadelphia to Erie and Pittsburgh to Stroudsburg. It took seven months to accomplish this goal while working our real jobs, trying to maintain our normal business travel schedule, and occasionally seeing our families and friends. At each winery we talked with the owner, the vineyard manager, the winemaker, and the salesroom staff, roles that are sometimes filled by one person or a couple. In total, we did fifty-four interviews. In one case, the winery closed after we visited; in another, the winery received its licensing and opened just before this book went to press.

The growing of grapes and the making of wine are processes that in principle require the same basic steps from one vineyard to another and one winery to another. The differences among wineries lie in the details of how the grapes are grown and the wines made. Our goal in interviewing the winery principals was to find out what made each winery unique. In the vineyard, there are a multitude of considerations and decisions—where to establish the vineyard, what grapes to grow, how to grow them. Winemaking decisions are equally complicated. The reasons for even starting in the business of growing grapes and/or making wine are as varied as the stories the different winery owners tell and the goals they ultimately would like to achieve. Every winery proved to be, indeed, unique.

In addition to this publication in print, two other versions of *Pennsylvania Wineries* exist: one on CD-ROM and another on the Internet, where the text will be updated frequently. Visit the website for this book at www.vitis-ir.com/pawine to obtain current information on new Pennsylvania wineries, changes in hours or in extension locations, and winery events and activities. The website gives the terms and conditions for a free trial subscription to the electronic version of *Pennsylvania Wineries.*

Visiting the wineries gave us the opportunity to take hundreds of photographs; some appear in the print version of this guide, and many more are available in color on the CD-ROM version of this book and at the book's website.

Driving to each winery allowed us to check out the directions we have included to be sure they are accurate and have the necessary details so that the wineries can be found as easily as possible. The maps for the wineries are drawn to show a winery's location in reference to major as well as local roads. Most wineries in Pennsylvania have adequate signage to help you find their location, and many use a common winery highway sign with a cluster of grapes.

We have tried to convey the character of each winery in our descriptions and to give you, the reader, a sense of what you'll find when you visit. Each winery has a separate chapter, arranged in alphabetical order for easy reference. In addition to the narrative description, each chapter gives the winery's location within the state; whether it belongs to a specific Wine Trail organization; its street address, phone and fax numbers, e-mail and website addresses; a list of the wines offered for sale, as well as the best-selling wine or wines; the hours the winery is open; information about any extensions the winery may have; and perhaps most important, written directions and a map.

Grapes in Pennsylvania

Grapes have been grown in Pennsylvania since the days of William Penn, and prior to Prohibition, the state had an active grape and wine industry. While some wineries in other states weathered Prohibition by making sacramental and medicinal wines, in Pennsylvania all the existing wineries closed. The grape industry survived, mostly because the majority of grapes grown in the state were either juice or table grapes.

Today Pennsylvania ranks fourth in the country in the number of tons of grapes produced. Most of the grapes, however, are grown for use by large companies such as Welch's for their juice products. It was not until the 1950s that some grape growers in Erie County began to experiment with growing wine grapes, and grape growing in the southeastern part of the state did not get started until the 1960s. When the Limited Winery Act allowing the existence of wineries in Pennsylvania was passed in 1968, new enthusiasm for growing grapes developed, and as more wineries opened, more vineyards were planted, which in turn led to more wineries.

Today's grape growers know that there are many different kinds of grapes that can be grown in Pennsylvania. Native American grapes, such as Concord and Niagara, can be grown throughout the state; French hybrid grapes, which are more cold and disease resistant, can be grown in Erie County, southeastern Pennsylvania, and certain microclimates in the mountains. The hybrid grapes were bred to take advantage of the disease and cold tolerance of the native grapes as well as the flavor and aroma characteristics of the vinifera grapes that have traditionally been made into premium table wines. The vinifera grapes—those grown in Europe, such as Chardonnay, Cabernet Sauvignon, and Merlot—are more difficult to grow in Pennsylvania, given the state's cold winters, spring frosts, and hot and humid summers.

Some winery owners think that growing vinifera grapes is a necessity in order to get their names on the map, whereas others think that it's more important for Pennsylvania to establish an identity based on quality wines from grapes of many different kinds. It will take many more years of growing grapes and making wine to determine exactly which grapes will produce the best wines in the different growing areas within Pennsylvania.

Viticulture in Pennsylvania

In order to make wine, a winemaker must first have grapes. Most wineries in Pennsylvania have vineyards. Those without vineyards must buy some or all the fruit they use.

There are many ways to get the vines in the ground, but the simplest method is to dig a hole and put in the vine. Some grape growers have developed ways to

Grape growers are hands-on farmers, as Tim Crouch demonstrates as he plants one of many vines at Allegro Vineyards in York County in the spring of 1999.

New vines planted during the spring of 1999 were protected by grow tubes at the Sunrise Vineyard, one of four different vineyards at Clover Hill Vineyards & Winery.

While most vineyards use wooden posts to support the trellis wires for vines, Big Creek Vineyard uses concrete posts made on the premises.

minimize the backbreaking part of planting. At Galen Glen Vineyard and Winery, Galen Troxell put his engineering background to work and designed a semi-automatic grape planter to help with planting his vineyard. It is just one example of ingenuity in the vineyard.

Some growers are using a new technique to help young and tender vines get established. "Grow tubes" provide a protected environment that encourages vines to grow quickly to the first wire of the trellis system. Most newly planted vineyards have wooden posts to support the trellis wires that will in turn support the vines. A unique solution to the problems of wooden posts was found by Dominic Strohlein, who makes his own posts out of concrete. These posts at Big Creek Vineyard do not need to be replaced as frequently as do wooden posts.

As grapes get ripe, the sugar content rises in the berries. When that happens, grapes become attractive to birds and other animals. A large flock of hungry birds can devour all of a vineyard's grapes in a very short time. One way to protect the grape crop is to cover the vines with netting to prevent birds from getting at the grapes. Cheryl Caplan at Twin Brook Winery covers all of the vines in her vineyard with bird netting (see photo on page 161). Deer also can be a problem, and Mark Gearhart at Evergreen Valley Vineyards uses a solar-powered electric fence to help keep deer out of the vineyard (see photo on page 51).

Harvesting grapes has been a labor-intensive process for thousands of years. Today, primarily because of the difficulty of finding labor to harvest the grapes, many vineyards use mechanical harvesters to provide a reliable and cost-effective way of bringing in the grapes.

Making Wine in Pennsylvania

Throughout the world, winemaking follows a similar sequence of steps, and the differences in what one winemaker does as compared to the next winemaker constitute the art of winemaking. Pennsylvania wineries range in size from very small, where less than 1,000 gallons of wine are produced, to those of medium size, which make between 30,000 and 75,000 gallons of wine. The facilities used as production plants for wineries vary as well. Many Pennsylvania wineries are housed in traditional Pennsylvania bank barns, such as at Pinnacle Ridge Winery (see photo on page 129). Bank barns have the advantage of being built into a hill, which allows for ground level access to at least two different levels of the barn. Occasionally new facilities will also utilize the environmental

Harvesting grapes at Nissley Vineyards.

advantages of having at least part of the winery building underground, as was the case at Stargazers Vineyard (see photo on page 154).

Because the size of the production in Pennsylvania's wineries varies, so does the equipment used by the wineries. A winery producing 1,000 gallons can use 5-gallon glass carboys and small-scale equipment, while wineries dealing with many tons of grapes must have larger equipment capable of crushing and pressing the grapes quickly and efficiently.

Once harvested, the grapes must be converted into wine. The first step in making white wine is to remove the stems and leaves, crush the fruit, and then separate the juice from the skins and seeds. The process of crushing the grapes should be a gentle one of just breaking the berries. The skins and seeds of the grapes are separated from the juice in a wine press. The fresh juice is then sent into the winery tank to be fermented. The yeast—either the "wild" yeast that exists on all grapes or yeast that the winemaker adds to control the fermentation—then does the difficult work of converting the sweet juice into wine.

To make red wines, the crushed grapes and their juice are pumped into a tank and, at the winemaker's discretion, yeast is added. After the red grape juice has fermented into wine, the young wine is separated

Aurore grapes are dumped into the crusher on their way to becoming wine at Nissley Vineyards.

Bill Gulvin, winemaker at Nissley Vineyards, prepares to empty the press that is full of Aurore grape skins.

The "tank farm" at Buckingham Valley Vineyards has what looks like a tank lying on its side. It is not a tank, but a rotary fermenter that is used primarily for making red wines.

from the skins and seeds, using the same press that was used to press the juice for white wines.

In wineries, a group of tanks holding the wines are sometimes called a "tank farm," or if in barrels, a barrel rack. The tank farm at Buckingham Valley Vineyards includes a new high-tech piece of equipment called a rotary fermenter. This fermenter works somewhat like a gentle cement mixer, as it mixes red grape skins and juice during fermentation to maximize the extraction of flavors and color from the grapes. At the other end of the spectrum are wineries, such as Presque Isle Wine Cellars, which use barrels, small-sized stainless steel tanks, and glass carboys to store their wine both during and after fermentation (see photo on page 133).

One of the important tools for winemakers is the wine laboratory. Sometimes this lab is limited to the kitchen counter, but in other wineries it can be as well equipped as the laboratory at Chaddsford Winery. Winemakers use their laboratories to analyze the constituents of grapes and wine, such as fruit acids, sugars, and alcohol levels. They also conduct trials in the lab to determine the various steps in winemaking, such as clar-

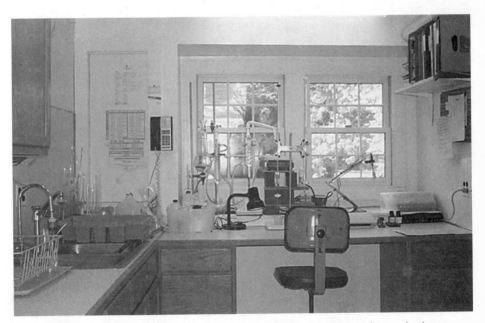

The laboratory at Chaddsford Winery is set up to allow the winemaker to check on the progress of any of the winery's wines.

When it is time to bottle wine at Calvaresi Winery, the stainless steel tank, at the top of this photo, is filled with wine, which then feeds by gravity through the four bottling spouts into empty bottles.

ifying or preserving the wine from spoilage. Lab tests help winemakers make good decisions both in the vineyard and in the wine cellar.

The final step in the winemaking process is to put the wine in the bottle so that the consumer can buy it and enjoy it. If this procedure is not done with appropriate care, the wine will quickly spoil. Smaller wineries use smaller equipment, such as the four-spout filler fed by a gravity tank that is used at Calvaresi Winery. On the other end of the spectrum is the totally automatic bottling line at The Winery at Wilcox (see photo on page 174).

When you visit wineries, ask to take their tour and watch how each winery handles the different steps in making wine. At first, all wineries may seem to be the same, but a closer look will tell you that they are quite different from one another. Look for signs of the ingenuity that the winemakers use to solve the many problems they face in making good wine from their grapes. Listen to the stories they tell of how they got into the industry and the problems and the fun they have doing what they do. Most winemakers love what they do, and are pleased to talk about it.

Most important, taste the wines at the wineries. Don't be afraid to try wines that are different from the kind of wine you think you like. You may be surprised by what you discover.

The Wine Areas of Pennsylvania

The wineries in Pennsylvania can be divided into three regions based on geography: the Lake Erie region, the mountains, and the southeast, as shown on the general maps. The Lake Erie area has the fewest wineries, only six, but more acres of grapes are grown there than in any other part of the state. Approximately 11,000 acres of vineyards grow along Lake Erie. While most of that acreage is planted with native American grapes such as

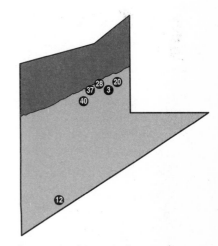

Lake Erie Wineries

❸ Arrowhead Wine Cellars
⓬ Conneaut Cellars Winery *
⓴ Heritage Wine Cellars
㉘ Mazza Vineyards *
㊲ Penn Shore Vineyards *
㊽ Presque Isle Wine Cellars *

* Lake Erie Quality Wine Alliance

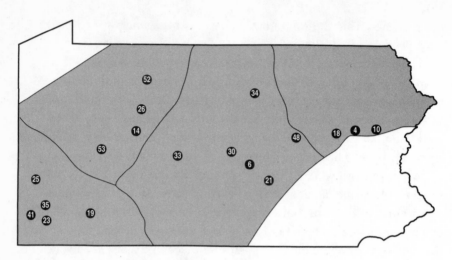

Mountain Wineries

Northwest Area
- ⑭ Evergreen Valley Vineyards
- ㉖ Laurel Mountain Vineyard
- ㉝ Windgate Vineyards
- ㉜ The Winery at Wilcox

Southwest Area
- ㉓ Christian W. Klay Winery
- ⑲ Glades Pike Winery
- ㉕ Lapic Winery
- ㉟ Paterini Winery
- ㊶ Quaker Ridge Winery

Northeast Area
- ❹ Big Creek Vineyard *
- ❿ Cherry Valley Vineyards *
- ⑱ Galen Glen Vineyard and Winery

Central Area
- ❻ Brookmere Farm Vineyards
- ㉑ Hunters Valley Winery
- ㉚ Mount Nittany Vineyard & Winery
- ㉝ Oak Spring Winery
- ㉞ Oregon Hill Winery
- ㊽ Susquehanna Valley Winery

* Lehigh Valley Wine Trail

Concord and Niagara, many acres of wine grapes are also grown there, and the grapes are sold to wineries across the state.

The southeastern part of Pennsylvania has the largest number of wineries, with twenty-nine. We have chosen to use the Appalachian Trail as the dividing line between the mountain region and the southeast. The trail runs along the ridge of hills farthest to the southeast in Pennsylvania. The vineyard acreage in the southeast has increased in recent years, and as premium grapes have become more difficult for wineries to purchase because of the increase in demand, more acreage will probably be planted in the near future. The climate, the topography, and the soils are

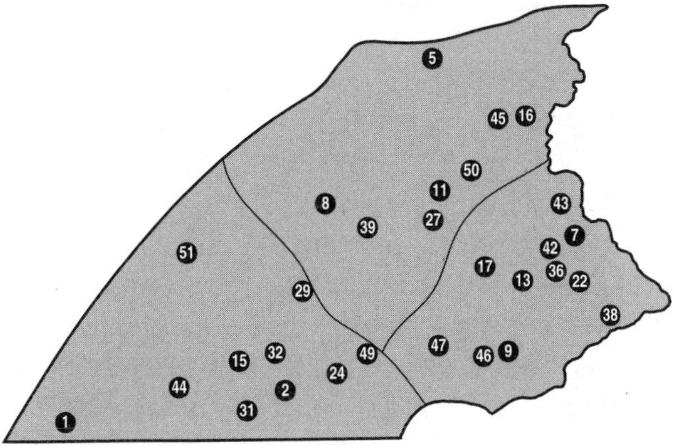

Southeast Wineries

Lehigh Valley

⑤ Blue Mountain Vineyards *
⑧ Calvaresi Winery
⑪ Clover Hill Vineyards & Winery *
⑯ Franklin Hill Vineyards *
㉗ Manatawny Creek Winery
㊴ Pinnacle Ridge Winery *
㊺ Slate Quarry Winery *
㊿ Vynecrest Winery *

Susquehanna Valley

① Adams County Winery
② Allegro Vineyards ††
⑮ Fox Ridge Vineyard and Winery
㉔ Lancaster County Winery
㉙ Mount Hope Estate & Winery
㉛ Naylor Wine Cellars ††
㉜ Nissley Vineyards
㊹ Seven Valleys Vineyard & Winery ††
㊾ Twin Brook Winery †
(51) West Hanover Winery

Philadelphia Area

⑦ Buckingham Valley Vineyards and Winery
⑨ Chaddsford Winery †
⑬ Country Creek Winery
⑰ French Creek Ridge Vineyards †
㉒ In & Out Farm Vineyards
㊱ Peace Valley Winery
㊳ Philadelphia Wine Company
㊷ Rushland Ridge Vineyards & Winery
㊸ Sand Castle Winery
㊻ Smithbridge Cellars †
㊼ Stargazers Vineyard †

---

* Lehigh Valley Wine Trail
† Chester County Wine Trail
†† Mason-Dixon Wine Trail

all conducive to growing grapes in the southeastern part of the state; the only limiting factor is the impingement of development from suburban and urban areas into more rural countryside.

In Pennsylvania the mountains cover the greatest amount of territory and offer significant challenges to those who want to grow grapes and make wine within the area. There are microclimates within this extensive region where grapes can grow quite nicely, especially if care is taken to choose varieties that are appropriate for cool-climate viticulture. Southern slopes, high ridges, good air drainage, the right soils, and favorable microclimates can allow vineyards to survive and produce quality wines. For the most part, however, wineries north of Interstate 80 in the mountains of Pennsylvania have found that they must purchase most, if not all, of their grapes.

The one disadvantage of dividing Pennsylvania into these three areas is that a winery near a border may be geographically in one region but also may be close to wineries in another region and participate in industry events with those wineries. When this is the case, we have listed the winery in the appropriate region but have also included its Wine Trail listing.

Tasting Pennsylvania's Wines

All of the wineries in Pennsylvania have tasting rooms where you can sample some or all of a winery's products. One of the most convenient ways to try wines from a number of different wineries is to attend a wine festival. Currently four major festivals are held in Pennsylvania:

- Art Craft Wine Festival, Bethlehem, early May.

- WineFest at the ArtsFest, Harrisburg, Memorial Day weekend in May.

- Great Tastes of Pennsylvania Wine and Food Festival, Split Rock Resort, Lake Harmony, the last weekend in June.

- Seven Springs Wine and Food Festival, Seven Springs Mountain Resort, Champion, mid-August.

There are several different ways to find out when these festivals and other events at individual wineries are happening. One is to check the Calendar of Events in *The Pennsylvania Wine Traveler*, the newspaper published by the Pennsylvania Wine Association and available for no charge at Pennsylvania State Stores. Or you can log on to one of the websites for wine, such as www.wineinfonet.com/pawine. In addition, the

Pennsylvania Wine Association has an executive director who can answer many questions or refer you to a specific source. Write to the Pennsylvania Wine Association, P.O. Box 2304, Sinking Spring, PA 19608, telephone (877) 4PA-WINE (toll-free) or (610) 927-2505, fax (610) 927-2506, or e-mail pawine@voicenet.com.

Visiting Pennsylvania's Wineries

It's possible to view the wineries in Pennsylvania as clusters, or groups, of wineries that can be visited in the course of a day or a weekend. There are three official Wine Trails: the Chester County Wine Trail; the Lehigh Valley Wine Trail, near Allentown; and the Mason-Dixon Wine Trail, which includes three wineries in southern York County plus three in Maryland (Boordy Vineyards, in Hydes, 410-592-5015; Fiore Winery, in Pylesville, 410-836-7605; and Woodhall Vineyards & Winecellars, in Parkton, 410-512-4598). The wineries near Lake Erie are organized into another interstate organization called the Lake Erie Quality Wine Alliance, which includes members in New York, Pennsylvania, and Ohio. For more information, contact the Alliance office at P.O. Box 10755, Erie, PA 16414, telephone (800) 600-WINE.

Wine lovers who live in or are visiting a certain part of the state and want to spend a day tasting Pennsylvania wines can visit a group of wineries in that area. For example, there are four wineries south of Pittsburgh, four near Du Bois, four near Harrisburg, and three not far from State College.

The maps on pages xxi–xxiii include all the wineries in Pennsylvania separated into the three major regions. Each major area is divided into smaller regions to help readers locate and plan winery visits.

🍇 Adams County Winery

251 Peach Tree Rd., Orrtanna, PA 17353
PHONE: (717) 334-4631
FAX: (717) 334-4026
E-MAIL: adamscountywinery@blazenet.net

LOCATION: Southeast, Susquehanna Valley

THE ADAMS COUNTY WINERY IS BOTH ONE OF PENNSYLVANIA'S OLDEST wineries and one of its newest. The original winery was founded by Ron and Ruth Cooper in 1975, but the current owners only purchased the winery late in September 1998.

The Coopers selected the location in the rolling, fruit-growing country of Adams County, northwest of Gettysburg, because of the deep soils, plentiful moisture, and cool nights, even in the summer. The winery was housed in a century-old barn, with the tasting room in one corner room of the ground floor and the winery facility in the other basement rooms. After about five years, the Coopers sold the winery to Tom and Beverly Campbell, who operated Adams County Winery as a retirement project for the next eighteen years. In 1998 they, too, decided it was time to sell the winery. On July 4, 1998, John Kramb and his wife, Katherine Bigler, happened to visit the winery and discovered that it was for sale.

John and Katherine both had been military officers in Washington, D.C., and their dream was to grow grapes and make wine. They were actively looking for a good location and thought they had found a wonderful site in North Carolina. Then they met the Campbells and saw Adams County Winery. John is a Civil War buff, and the idea of living so near to Gettysburg had great appeal. Katherine has family in Ohio and Rhode Island, and Pennsylvania seemed much closer to relatives than North Carolina. After doing some research and developing a business plan, the couple reached an agreement with the Campbells and purchased the winery on September 30, 1998, in the middle of harvest. Tom Campbell actually made almost all of the wine from the 1998 vintage and has agreed to be John's mentor and chief consultant.

To John and Katherine, Adams County Winery is a brand new experience. Several wines were sold out when they purchased the winery, and

1

The door on the far left of this century-old barn not far from Gettysburg leads to the tasting room for Adams County Winery.

until the new wine is ready, they don't know exactly what the wines they make will taste like. As new grape growers and winemakers, they have yet to experience the full-year vineyard and winery cycle. John planted somewhat less than an acre of Niagara grapes in the spring of 1999 and can envision expanding the vineyard to 10 or 12 acres. He plans to increase the output of the winery from the 2,300 gallons made in the fall of 1998 to perhaps 10,000 gallons, depending on the growth of the customer base, which is a mix of tourists to the Gettysburg area and local people.

The vineyard was originally planted by Ron and Ruth Cooper in 1974, with a variety of vinifera and French hybrid grapes. Today there are approximately 5 acres of Seyval, Vidal, Chardonnay, Foch, and Chancellor, and many of the vines were part of the original vineyard. The farm also includes 11 acres of apple orchards; some of the apples are used for the winery's apple wines.

John and Katherine have added some unique handmade pottery from the Shenandoah Valley in Virginia to the line of wine merchandise, such as bottle stoppers and wine bags, that they sell in the tasting room. Katherine is developing a series of computer-generated specialized labels and will offer private labeling for customers in the near future.

The wines sold at Adams County for this year are the result of the product mix developed by the previous owners. As John and Katherine develop their own plans and goals, the wines available may change to a certain extent.

PENNSYLVANIA
TABLE WINE
Tears of Gettysburg
First bottled in 1988 in honor of the
125th Anniversary of the Battle of Gettysburg
CONTAINS SULFITES
PRODUCED AND BOTTLED
BY ADAMS COUNTY WINERY
251 PEACH TREE RD., ORRTANNA, PA 17353

Wine List

Dry: Dry Red (Foch and Chancellor), Vidal Blanc, Seyval, Pinot Chardonnay, Pinot Gris, Cabernet Sauvignon, Red Red Wine (Foch and Chambourcin)

Semidry: Vidal Blanc, Seyval

Semisweet: Wisp O'The Vine (Niagara blend)

Sweet: 3 Ships to the Wind (Foch plus citrus extract), Apple, Adam's Apple (Apple plus cinnamon and other spices), Sweet Scarlet, Tears of Gettysburg (Niagara blend), Rascal Red Sweet (red blend with spices), Rhedd Butler (Foch and Chardonnay)

Best-selling Wine: Tears of Gettysburg (Niagara blend)

Hours

January–March, weekends and holidays, noon to 6:00 P.M. April–December, every day except Wednesday, noon to 6:00 P.M.

Directions

Go west from Gettysburg 8 miles on Route 30 West. Turn left on High Street toward Cashtown (and away from the Round Barn). Turn left at the stop sign, go 100 yards, and turn right on Orrtanna Road. At the stop sign in 1 mile, turn right, then veer left immediately onto Scott School Road. Go 1/2 mile, and turn right on Peach Tree Road. Turn left in 1/2 mile; the winery is at the end of the driveway. Though these directions may sound complex, the signage is excellent at every turn.

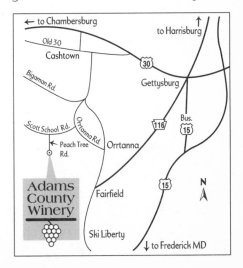

🍇 Allegro Vineyards

3475 Sechrist Rd., Brogue, PA 17309
PHONE: (717) 927-9148
E-MAIL: info@allegrowines.com
WEBSITE: www.allegrowines.com

LOCATION: Southeast, Susquehanna Valley
(Mason-Dixon Wine Trail)

WHEN TIM AND JOHN CROUCH, BOTH MUSICIANS, OPENED THEIR WINERY in 1980, they chose to call it Allegro, a name that reflected their interest in classical music. (Tim played the violin and John the oboe.) Over the years a number of their wines have also had names with a musical connection, such as their premium Cabernet Sauvignon, which is currently called Cadenza. In the early 1980s the brothers produced a blend of Seyval Blanc and Peach wine and received Bureau of Alcohol, Tobacco, and Firearms (BATF) approval to call it Opus 1 in February 1983.

Also in the early 1980s Robert Mondavi and Baron Phillippe Rothschild went into partnership in California to produce a premium red

wine. It took more than two years for the partnership to come up with a name for the wine that would be unique and reflect the image they perceived for their wine. The name they chose, Opus One, was not released until November 1983, after regis-

The label at the top of the Gai corking machine is for Allegro Vineyard's Opus 1, a blend of Seyval and Peach wines that was made in the early 1980s before Robert Mondavi and Baron Philippe Rothschild named their premium red wine Opus One. The corker was purchased with some of the money the Crouches received as settlement from the Mondavi/Rothschild group for the use of the name Opus One.

tered trademark proceedings were finished. At that point, the Mondavi-Rothschild group found that this name was already in use by Allegro Vineyards. After some discussion between lawyers for the two wineries, John and Tim agreed to stop using the name Opus on their wine in return for a cash settlement. With some of those funds, they purchased a Gai corker, which they continue to use. It is still in the winery, with a faded but still legible label for Allegro's Opus 1 decorating the front of the machine. John's only disappointment about this episode in the winery's history is that Robert Mondavi never visited Allegro to taste and exchange wines, which John thinks would have been good publicity for both wineries.

The original vineyard at Allegro was planted in 1973, and many of the Cabernet vines were part of that original vineyard. The Crouches bought the property in 1978 and now have a total of 12 acres planted primarily with Seyval and Chardonnay. A small amount of additional fruit is purchased from nearby growers, including one vineyard, the James Vineyard, that will be recognized on the label for the next release of Cabernet Sauvignon.

Both John and Tim Crouch realize that they are better at growing grapes and making good wine than they are at marketing. While they do not particularly want to be in the entertainment business, as they describe it, over the years they have developed a popular series of dinners that they call the Chef Series. On five Thursday evenings from late May to mid-August, they bring a well-known and well-respected local chef to the winery to match Allegro wines with an outdoor gourmet dinner for eighty people. The winery sells wine, the restaurant gets good publicity, and the guests have an excellent meal at a reasonable price—and get to take the recipes home with them. The chefs for the 1999 dinners came from restaurants in York, Lancaster, and Harrisburg. Recipes featuring Allegro wines can also be found on the winery's website.

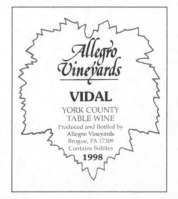

Wine List

Dry: Chardonnay, Chardonnay Reserve, Proprietor's White (Chardonnay and Seyval), Proprietor's Special Selection Red (Cabernet Sauvignon, Chambourcin, Chelois, and Léon

Millot), James Vineyard Cabernet Sauvignon, Cadenza (Cabernet Sauvignon Reserve), Premium Red (Chambourcin, Chelois, and Léon Millot)

Semidry: Premium White (Seyval and Vidal), Riesling

Semisweet: Vidal, Brogue Blush

Sweet: Celeste (Peach and Seyval), Apple, Cherry

Best-selling Wine: Vidal

Hours

Friday–Sunday, noon to 5:00 P.M. (Other hours by appointment.)

Services and Events

Picnic area, Chef Series of dinners, Spotlight weekends (wine and food matching and tasting), Case Club, Nouveau weekend, Christmas open house.

Directions

From York, take I-83 South to exit 6E. Go east on Route 74 to Brogue. Follow the big blue Allegro signs, and turn right on Muddy Creek Road (watch for signs for Muddy Creek; when we visited, there was no sign for the road itself). Go 2 miles to Sechrist Road. Turn left on Sechrist; the driveway entrance for the winery is on the left at the bottom of the hill.

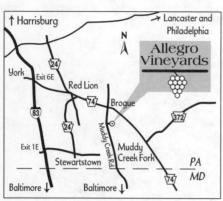

Arrowhead Wine Cellars

12703 East Main Rd., North East, PA 16428
PHONE: (814) 725-5509
FAX: (814) 725-8904

LOCATION: **Lake Erie**

ARROWHEAD WINE CELLARS OFFICIALLY STARTED BUSINESS ON JULY 1, 1999, and consequently, at the time of publication of this book, is the most recent winery to open in Pennsylvania. For many years, Nick and Kathy Mobilia, grape growers in North East, have been supplying wine grapes in the form of bulk juice to wineries in five states from their 100-acre farm. This past year, their son Adrian graduated from Pennsylvania State University with a degree in horticulture. As a result, Nick decided to expand the family business to include a winery so that there would be a niche for Adrian, who is now managing the vineyard.

Another partner in the winery is Pat Murphy, who has twenty-five years of management experience. His son Jeff graduated in 1999 from Penn State with a degree in food science and will be making the wine.

Nick and Kathy have been selling fresh and pick-your-own fruit for many years, and they turned half of their fresh fruit stand into the winery facility. The fruit stand and winery has an excellent location near an exit of I-90, and the Mobilia farm is actually split by the highway.

The Mobilia farm has 100 acres planted in grapes, plus more acreage devoted to fruit crops such as apples and cherries. The grape varieties currently planted are Concord, Niagara, Catawba, Steuben, Delaware, and Chambourcin. Other kinds of grapes will be added to improve the varietal mix for the winery in the near future, including Riesling and Cabernet Franc in the spring of 2000.

7

Wine List

Dry: Chardonnay, Riesling, Delaware, Chambourcin

Semidry: Buffalo Blush (Buffalo, Steuben)

Semisweet: Niagara, Fredonia, Cherry

Sweet: Pink Catawba, Concord

Hours

Monday–Saturday, 10:00 A.M. to 6:00 P.M. (8:00 P.M. late summer to early fall); Sunday, noon to 6:00 P.M.

Services and Events

Fruit stand with fresh fruits and vegetables.

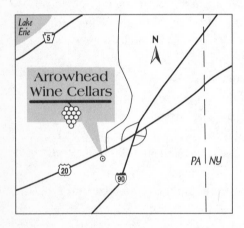

Directions

Take Exit 12 from I-90 and go west on Route 20 about 1/4 mile. The winery is past the McDonald's and 84 Lumber on the left.

🍇 Big Creek Vineyard

R.R. 5, Box 5270, Kunkletown, PA 18058
PHONE: (610) 681-3959
FAX: (610) 681-3960
E-MAIL: bigcreek@ptd.prolog.net

LOCATION: **Mountains, Northeast Area**
(Lehigh Valley Wine Trail)

WHILE DOMINIC STROHLEIN WAS WORKING ON HIS PH.D. IN VETERINARY parasitology, he learned to cook. His interest in good food led to an interest in wine, which then led to learning how to make wine. As his interest in wine grew stronger, he began to plan for a career not in a laboratory, but in a winery.

Every summer while Dominic was growing up in Brooklyn, he would visit his grandparents on their 80-acre farm just over the first mountain ridge north of Allentown. After becoming interested in wine, he traveled to wineries from Virginia to New York to find out what grapes were being grown and what wines the winemakers were making. He decided that although the family farm might not be quite as far south or as close to sea level as he would have liked, it did have three advantages: the cost was right, it was available, and it had approximately 25 acres that could be planted with grapes.

The winery became a family affair in other ways as well. Dominic's mother, Mildred, helps run the tasting room at the winery and at the extension in Jim Thorpe. His brother, Stephen, is planning to join the winery full-time soon, and Stephen's wife, Annette, may also come on board.

Big Creek Vineyard is in an area Dominic describes as the foothills of the Pocono Mountains or the gateway to the Poconos. The name Big Creek is the translation for the word the Indians used for the area, *pohopoco*, and is the name for the stream that runs near the winery. A large development of second homes is located nearby, and as a result, most of the winery's business starts with Memorial Day weekend and goes through the holidays in December. Dominic also decided to open an extension where there were more people on a regular basis. He chose

Fermentation locks on top of each barrel allow gases to escape as the wine ferments at Big Creek Vineyard. In the background, winemaker Dominic Strohlein talks with author Richard Carey.

the town of Jim Thorpe, formerly a coal-mining town but now a tourist center with antiques stores, art galleries, and cafés.

If you look carefully at the vineyard, you'll see one aspect that is different from most other vineyards in the United States. In this country, most grape growers use wooden posts, but Dominic didn't like having to deal with truckloads of wood, so he decided to try another way. Since he has a local source for concrete, he designed the forms to pour his own posts and now can make them out of reinforced concrete whenever he needs more (see page xiv).

The winery opened in 1996, and by 1998 half of the 20-acre vineyard was producing grapes. Dominic made 5,000 gallons during the 1998 harvest and, as more vines come into production, will continue to increase the winery's production. The winery building was designed to allow for expansion to about 12,000 gallons. A large area beyond the tasting room is planned for case storage in the future. Until it is needed, Dominic uses the area as an artists' gallery and for special events.

BIG CREEK VINEYARD

PRODUCED & BOTTLED BY BIG CREEK VINEYARD, LTD.
KUNKLETOWN, PENNSYLVANIA

1998
CARMÉ
DRY WHITE TABLE WINE
750 ML

Wine List

Dry: Seyval, Chambourcin, Pinot Noir, Cabernet (Cabernet Sauvignon and Cabernet Franc), Sangiovese/Dolcetto

Semidry: Vin di Pasqualina (Vidal, Chambourcin, and Niagara), Carmé (Chardonnay plus some Malvasia Bianca and Muscat Blanc)

Semisweet: Dulcinea (Seyval)

Sparkling and Fruit Wines: Sparkling Raspberry, Spiced Hard Cider, Dry Apple Wine, Sweet Apple Wine

Best-selling Wine: Dulcinea

Hours

Monday–Thursday, 1:00 to 5:00 P.M.; Friday–Saturday, 1:00 to 7:00 P.M.; Sunday, 2:00 to 5:00 P.M.

Services and Events

Custom labels.

Directions

From Route 33, take Route 209 west to Route 534 in Kresgeville. Turn right onto Route 534 West, and go 0.1 mile to Beltzville Road. Turn left and go 1.3 miles to Keller Road. Turn left onto Keller and go 0.3 mile to the second driveway on the left.

Extension

53 Race St., Jim Thorpe, (570) 325-8138 (open Monday–Thursday, 1:00 to 5:00 P.M.; Friday–Saturday, 1:00 to 6:00 P.M.; Sunday, 2:00 to 5:00 P.M.).

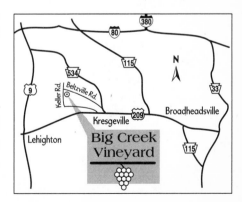

Blue Mountain Vineyards

7627 Grape Vine Dr., P.O. Box 492, New Tripoli, PA 18066
PHONE: (610) 298-3068
FAX: (610) 298-8616
E-MAIL: bmvsales@bmvc.com
WEBSITE: www.bmvc.com

LOCATION: **Southeast, Lehigh Valley**
(Lehigh Valley Wine Trail)

BLUE MOUNTAIN VINEYARDS IS NOT THE OLDEST OR THE NEWEST WINERY in Pennsylvania, but it may be the one that plans to grow the fastest. When the winery first opened only six years ago, the vineyard had 9 producing acres, and all the wine—2,000 gallons—was made in Joe and Vickie Greff's garage. By 1999 the Greffs owned two farms, had 25 producing acres, and planted a total of 15 acres of new vines in the spring of 1999. As the number of acres producing grapes increases, Joe and Vickie plan to expand the winery, with their next goal being 25,000 gallons. They can foresee the day when the winery will produce more than 100,000 gallons, but they want to produce all the fruit used in their wines so that the wines are truly an estate-produced product, and the size of the winery will depend on the amount of fruit they can harvest from their vineyards.

The Greffs bought their first farm in the early 1980s, with the idea that they might grow some grapes as a hobby. After talking with other vineyard owners, reading widely, and visiting wineries in California and Europe, the Greffs melded the various ideas into a plan for their property and planted the first vines in 1986. Joe's original plan was to sell the grapes to other wineries, but gradually he became more interested in making his own wine, and the project began to look more like a potential business than a hobby. By 1992, 9 acres on the farm were producing, and the Greffs opened Blue Mountain Vineyards in 1993 with a production of 2,000 gallons that were made in the Greffs' garage.

Two years later, a new winery building was ready in time for harvest, and the Greffs were fully launched into new careers—Joe as winemaker, and Vickie as sales and marketing manager for the winery. By 1998 25 acres of vineyard were in production and the volume of wine produced had grown to 12,000 gallons.

In January 1999 the Greffs bought another farm with 80 acres several miles north of the original farm. They planted 15 of those acres in the spring with Riesling, Chardonnay, Syrah, Cabernet Sauvignon, Cabernet Franc, Merlot, and Chambourcin. The new farm, which the Greffs are calling Leaser Lake Vineyards, dates back to the time of the American Revolution, when it was owned by Fredrick Leaser. Leaser made a place for himself in the history books by offering to transport the Liberty Bell from Philadelphia to a church in Allentown to protect it from the British.

Because the farm has historic significance, the Greffs started an Adopt a Vine program that allows customers to adopt a piece of that history. For a fee, a customer adopts a vine or vines and in return receives a special invitation to attend the opening of the restored Leaser home-stead, an opportunity to purchase shares of stock at a preoffering price when the winery is taken public (at some point in the future), and per-haps most importantly, bottles of wine of that varietal with personalized labels.

The current building housing Blue Mountain Vineyards was specifically designed to be a winery. The wine cellar's 15-foot-high ceilings and 14-inch-thick concrete walls help maintain an even temperature for the wines. The building is built into the hill, so the winery level is accessible to the drive outside, while cus-tomers can walk into the tasting room above from the parking lot.

Vickie and Joe Greff stand on their unfinished new deck outside the tasting room overlooking both the vineyards and the pond beside the win-ery. Joe had just come in from the vineyard where he had been using the plastic green ties in his waist pouch to fasten vines to the trellis wires.

The tasting room on the level above the winery is a large, open space with wooden beams and windows looking down toward the pond. During the winter of 1998–99, the Greffs enclosed the deck looking over the vineyard toward the mountains and added two wood-burning stoves for heat so that special events can be held there no matter what the weather. Another deck has been built overlooking the pond and will be available for summertime events.

Vickie feels strongly that visiting a winery should be more than tasting wine; she sees it as an experience, and it should be fun. Consequently, she plans many different types of events and encourages groups such as the Make-a-Wish Foundation and the Leukemia Society to hold special benefits at the winery. She has planned a range of barrel tastings, music, art, and food events to appeal to a wide variety of customers.

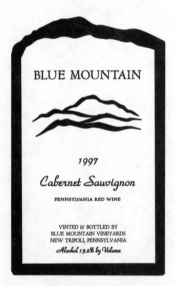

BLUE MOUNTAIN

1997

Cabernet Sauvignon

PENNSYLVANIA RED WINE

VINTED & BOTTLED BY
BLUE MOUNTAIN VINEYARDS
NEW TRIPOLI, PENNSYLVANIA
Alcohol 13.2% by Volume

Wine List

Dry: Vidal Blanc, Chardonnay, Chambourcin, Chambourcin Reserve, Nouveau Boujolais (Gamay), Pinot Noir, Merlot, Cabernet Sauvignon, Cabernet Sauvignon Reserve, Blue Heron Meritage (Merlot, Cabernet Sauvignon, and Cabernet Franc), Cabernet Franc

Semidry: Riesling, Vignoles

Semisweet: Mountain Breeze (Seyval, Chambourcin for color)

Sweet: Mountain Frost (Vidal), Late Harvest Vignoles, Bri's Blush (Vignoles, Chambourcin for color), Victoria's Passion (Chambourcin), Mountain Spice (blend of six apple varieties)

Best-selling Wines: Merlot, Blue Heron Meritage

Hours

Monday–Friday, 4:00 to 7:00 P.M.; Saturday–Sunday, 10:00 A.M. to 6:00 P.M.

Services and Events

Indoor and outdoor decks, Wine Club, Adopt a Vine Program, custom labeling, music and arts events.

Directions

From Route 22 west of Allentown, take Route 100 north towards Route 309. Turn left on Holbens Valley Road. In 2.2 miles, turn right onto Schochary Road. Go 2 miles, and turn left on Grape Vine Drive. The winery is on the right.

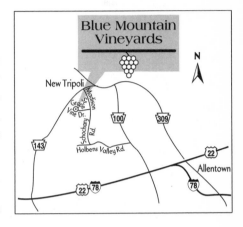

Extensions

Open only during the Christmas season.

Brookmere Farm Vineyards

5369 S.R. 655, Belleville, PA 17004
PHONE: (717) 935-5380
FAX: (717) 935-5349
WEBSITE: www.villagehost.com/brookmere

LOCATION: **Mountains, Central Area**

WHEN ASKED WHAT HE DID FOR A LIVING BEFORE RUNNING A WINERY, Don Chapman replies quickly, "I was a forger." After the listener's chin drops, Don then explains that he was a forger—of hot metal. He came to Lewistown from Connecticut in 1966 to merge two companies together and stayed to grow grapes and open a winery.

When Don and his wife, Susan, moved to the area, they bought a 138-acre farm. Don began to consider the possibility of making wine and tried to purchase the Lembo's Vineyards in Lewistown. Joe and Antoinette Lembo had developed a loyal following for their winery, which was located in a row house. As the Lembos grew older, they thought about selling the winery several times. Don was the fourth person to make an offer, and he began to work with Larry Smith, who helped make the wine for the Lembos, in anticipation of taking over the winery. When the Lembos decided not to sell, Don redirected his efforts toward converting his barn into a winery. He continued to work with Larry, but the wines they made were for Brookmere Farm Vineyards.

The Chapmans planted 3 acres of vineyard in 1982 and in the years since have expanded the vineyard to more than 5 acres. Don is growing Vidal, Seyval, Chelois, Chardonel, Chambourcin, and some Cabernet Sauvignon, and he plans to add some DeChaunac. Over the years, he has found that the vinifera such as Chardonnay do not grow well on his site, and also that the majority of his customers prefer sweeter wines that are made from grapes other than the vinifera. The vineyards are located on two sites on his property, both with good air drainage down to Frog Hollow Run, a little stream that runs through the farm.

The bank barn used by Brookmere was built in 1866 close to the road, which is now a well-traveled highway. Good signs and location help bring people to the winery, and over the years, the Chapmans have developed a following for their wines. The winery is now a local land-mark, partly because people like the wines, and also because the staff is friendly and trained to serve their customers' needs and preferences.

Some barns adapt to winery use more easily than others, and the Chapmans were lucky with theirs. They were able to put in a concrete floor and floor drains, and had enough ceiling height for stainless steel tanks. There is room for the winery facility, some case storage, and a pleasant tasting room. The winery opened in 1984 and now produces 8,000 gallons. Don handles the vineyard and the winemaking, Susan does the books, and daughter Amy works part-time as well. Don has an engineering background, but he finds running a winery more fun than plant management.

Don views service and education as two of the most important aspects of a well-run winery. He and the tasting room manager, Linn Irvin, have trained the tasting room staff to be both knowledgeable and helpful. Central Pennsylvania wine drinkers and most transient travelers are not known for liking dry wines, and the customers at Brookmere reflect that.

Don and Susan Chapman's Victorian-style house, built in 1866, is located between the vineyards (on the right) and the winery.

Don makes some dry wines, including some vinifera wines from grapes purchased outside central Pennsylvania, but the majority of the wines have some sweetness.

The Vintners Loft, located upstairs in the barn, displays works for sale by local artists, artisans, and photographers.

Wine List

Dry: Valley Mist (Vidal, Seyval, and Chardonel), Valley Mist Reserve (Vidal, Seyval, and Chardonel), Chardonnay, Autumn Red (Chelois and DeChaunac), Chambourcin, Cabernet Sauvignon, Big Valley Spumante

Semidry: Riesling, Indian Summer (Riesling and Chardonnay), Autumn Red Semi-dry (Chelois and DeChaunac), Chambourcin Semi-dry

Semisweet: Chablis (primarily Vidal plus some Seyval), Rosé (Chelois), Tears of the Goose (primarily Chelois, plus Seyval, Vidal, and Chardonel), Apple

Sweet: Autumn Gold (Vidal and Seyval), Niagara, Shawnee Red (DeChaunac and Concord), Strawberry, Frog Hollow (Niagara and Chardonel), Strawberry Spumante, Niagara Spumante, Blueberry Spumante

Best-selling Wine: Niagara, Shawnee Red

Hours

Monday–Saturday, 10:00 A.M. to 5:00 P.M.; Sunday, 1:00 to 4:00 P.M. (Winter hours subject to change. Private tastings and winery tours by appointment.)

Services and Events

Custom labeling, art gallery. The Chapmans have used their Federal-style home next door to the winery as a bed and breakfast in the past and may reopen the B&B in the future.

Directions

Brookmere is located in the center of Pennsylvania, just north of Lewistown and not far from State College. Take Route 322 north from Lewistown to Route 655; a very large, green highway sign for the winery indicates which exit to take. At the bottom of the ramp, turn left (west) on Route 655. The winery is on the right in approximately 5 miles.

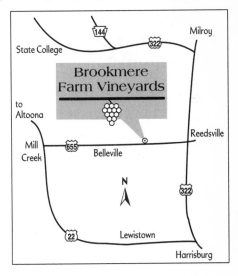

Buckingham Valley Vineyards and Winery

1521 Route 413, P.O. Box 371, Buckingham, PA 18912
PHONE: (215) 794-7188
FAX: (215) 794-3606
E-MAIL: gcforest@comcat.com
WEBSITE: vitis-ir.com/wineassn.

LOCATION: Southeast, Philadelphia Area

AT THE UNIVERSITY OF PENNSYLVANIA IN THE 1950S, JERRY FOREST AND his good friend Vladimir Guerrero played guitars and drank wine while dreaming about which of these activities they would pursue for a living. When reality hit, they decided they would have a better chance making wine. The two planted 5 acres of grapes in 1966 and resumed playing guitar and drinking wine (and earning a living doing other things) while the vines began to grow. In 1970 Jerry and his wife, Kathy, bought total control of the vineyards and in June 1973 opened Buckingham Valley Vineyards and Winery. From less than 1,000 gallons of wine produced that year, the winery has grown to 30,000 gallons, with fermenting and aging capacity of over 75,000 gallons. The original 5-acre site has expanded, through several acquisitions, to more than 40 acres. The family has grown, too, and the Forests' sons, Jon, Kevin, and Chris, are now a vital part of the operation of the vineyards and winery.

Although the winery has grown dramatically, the Forests have retained their laid-back attitude: no budgets, quotas, debt, or staff—just family and friends; no distributors or outlets—all the wine is sold at the winery; no formal guided tours; and no charge for visiting or tasting.

The Forests recognize that great wines start in the vineyard, and in Bucks County the growing conditions rival the best in the world. With fertile, well-drained limestone soil, moderate year-round temperatures, and good average monthly rainfall, the area is blessed with no floods, no earthquakes, no need for irrigation, and few blistering summers or vine-

Producing sparkling wine is a labor-intensive process, especially for small wineries. At Buckingham Valley Vineyards, Jerry Forest has automated the process using small-sized equipment imported from France. This machine replaces any wine that has been lost when the sediment has been removed from the neck of the bottle.

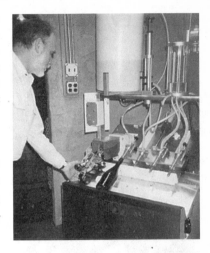

injuring winters. The 18 acres of vineyards are planted with eight varieties of French hybrids, vinifera, and native American grapes. New plantings will take place slowly until another 4 or 5 acres are under vine.

In the traditional method of making sparkling wine, the wine goes through a second fermentation in the bottle. During the fermentation process, the bottles are placed in a riddling rack. Over a period of time, the winemaker manually shakes the bottles to move yeast cells into the neck of the bottle. Once collected, they can be removed and the bottle properly corked.

A less time-consuming way to riddle sparkling wines is to place the bottles in a gyro-palette, such as this one at Buckingham Valley Vineyards, which automatically rotates the bin containing the sparkling wine bottles and settles the sediment into the neck of each bottle.

The grapes are harvested during September and early October with a French-built Braud mechanical harvester, which shakes the ripe grape berries off the vines and deposits them into a stainless steel gondola. Jerry Forest prefers this method over handpicking for several reasons: The harvester, which needs only a few people to operate, makes it possible to pick in the cool early morning and the grapes don't have to wait, sitting in the sun for hours, before they are collected and taken to the winery. Instead, the grapes are processed within minutes of picking.

The white wine grapes are pressed as quickly as possible after picking to preserve their fresh flavors and light color. Red wine grapes are fermented on their skins long enough to extract the desired color and complexity before being pressed. Most wines at Buckingham Valley spend their first year in stainless steel tanks and are racked (or transferred) from one tank to another several times in order to leave the sediment behind. The white and rosé wines are bottled after one or two years; the red wines are aged in oak for a longer time before being bottled and released. The Forests use state-of-the-art equipment, including a Europress membrane press, a rotary fermenter, a Pedia heat exchanger, cross-flow membrane filtration, and a Gai twelve-spout bottling line that cleans the bottles, sparges them with nitrogen, and fills, corks, capsules, and labels forty bottles per minute. It is this automation that has allowed Buckingham Valley to maintain its family-only policy for its work force. Outside help is used only for part-time wine shop sales and for pruning the vineyard.

Recently, the Forests added small-scale sparkling wine equipment, including an automatic riddling rack that turns the bottles to settle out the sediment, a dosage filler, and an automatic corker and wire hooder machine.

At Buckingham Valley, wine is considered to be a food, whether it is enjoyed with an actual meal or not. According to the Forests, wine should be consumed without ceremony or snobbery and should be affordable on an everyday basis. Consequently, the tasting room features pour-your-own tasting samples into real wine glasses, picnic tables, and most important, drinkable wines at reasonable prices.

There are more than a dozen varieties of wine, ranging from deep, oak-aged reds to light whites, from completely dry to fairly sweet. While most of the wines are made from grapes, the Forests also make apple, strawberry, and raspberry wines.

Wine List

Dry: Chardonnay, Vidal Blanc, Seyval Blanc, Nouveau (whole berry fermentation of Chambourcin, available in November and December only), DeChaunac, Chancellor, Rosette, Naturel Sparkling Wine (Vidal and Chardonnay), Chambourcin

Semidry: Nouvelle (predominantly Cayuga, available in November and December only), Riesling, Brut Sparkling Wine (Vidal, some Chardonnay and Cayuga)

Semisweet: First Blush (Vidal, Cayuga, and DeChaunac), Country Red (Foch)

Sweet: Niagara, White Sangria (mostly Niagara), Red Sangria (traditionally Foch), Concordia (Concord)

ROSETTE
Dry Table Wine

Produced and bottled for sale in Pennsylvania only by
Buckingham Valley Vineyards
1521 Route 413, Buckingham, Pa. 18912. Phone: 215-794-7188
This wine is made by traditional methods, patiently aged, and bottled when it reaches maturity. We hope you enjoy drinking our wine as much as we enjoy growing and making it.
The Forest Family

GOVERNMENT WARNING: (1) ACCORDING TO THE SURGEON GENERAL, WOMEN SHOULD NOT DRINK ALCOHOLIC BEVERAGES DURING PREGNANCY BECAUSE OF THE RISK OF BIRTH DEFECTS. (2) CONSUMPTION OF ALCOHOLIC BEVERAGES IMPAIRS YOUR ABILITY TO DRIVE A CAR OR OPERATE MACHINERY AND MAY CAUSE HEALTH PROBLEMS.

Fruit Wines: Apple, Raspberry, Strawberry

Best-selling Wines: Vidal, Blush, Chancellor

Hours

Tuesday–Saturday, 11:00 A.M. to 6:00 P.M.; Sunday, noon to 4:00 P.M.

Services and Events

Specialty labels, picnic facilities, duck pond.

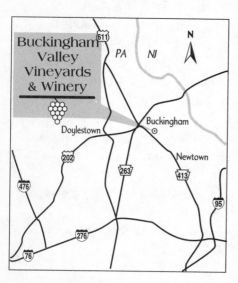

Directions

Buckingham Valley Vineyards is located on the east side of Route 413, 2 miles south of Route 202 and 8 miles north of Newtown.

 Calvaresi Winery

107 Shartlesville Rd., Bernville, PA 19506
PHONE: (610) 488-7966
FAX: (610) 488-1176
E-MAIL: dcalvaresi@aol.com

LOCATION: **Southeast, Lehigh Valley**

LIKE MANY WINEMAKERS, TOM CALVARESI FIRST STARTED MAKING WINE IN his basement at home. After more than ten years as a home winemaker, he converted the basement of his row house in Reading into a commercial winery and opened to the public in 1981 with the help (and tolerance) of his wife, Debbie. The winery had an initial production of 600 gallons and in three years grew to 3,000 gallons. Basements are often not ideal spaces for making wine: Tom's was long and narrow and lacked working space, room for expansion, and a place for customers to taste and enjoy his wines. In addition, Tom did not have a vineyard and purchased all his grapes and other fruit.

Tom and Debbie began to look for a property where they could build a winery with more ideal conditions for making wine. They found a location just outside of Bernville, a small town 10 miles northwest of Reading, with space for a winery, a parking lot, a house, and someday, a vineyard of 4 or 5 acres. It was close enough to Reading to be accessible to their existing customers but also offered much-needed space and a chance to expand their customer base.

The winery, designed to be all on one level, was completed in August 1988, in time for harvest. The juice or grapes come in at one end of the building, and there is plenty of space at this end of the building for all the basic winemaking tasks: crushing, destemming, pressing, fermenting. As the winemaking process progresses, the wine moves closer to the tasting room end of the building. It is a spacious and spotlessly clean facility, with room to walk between the tanks and kegs. Bottling takes place near the tasting room, and cases of wine are stored nearby. There are windows to let in the light, and a local artist has painted grapevines around them

Tom Calvaresi raises the lid of a plastic fermenting tank to check the fermentation progress of one of his red wines at Calvaresi Winery.

to add a touch of the outdoors on the inside. This is all quite a change from working in a cramped, dark basement.

While Tom is currently producing about 8,000 gallons, he has room within the winery to expand. And if necessary, he can add onto the production end of the building either to create a larger crushing pad or to expand his storage capacity.

Tom's customers in Berks County prefer wines with some sweetness, and he has always made sweet wines from native American grapes and slightly drier wines from some of the hybrid varietals. He continues to make a number of fruit wines in small quantities and in recent years has added two dry wines, a Pinot Gris and a Cabernet Franc.

The tasting room at Calvaresi is in one corner of the winery building. The slate floor defines the tasting area, which is open on one side to a view of the tanks and processing area of the winery and is separated from the bottling and wine storage area by a latticework "wall" on the other. A table displays various wine accessories for sale.

Wine List

Dry: Pinot Gris, Cabernet Franc

Semidry: Cayuga, Riesling, Baco Noir

Semisweet: Steuben Blush (formerly Widow's Blush)

Sweet: Niagara, Concord

Fruit Wines (in Season): Strawberry, Cherry, Apple, Blueberry, Blackberry, Raspberry, Peach

Best-selling Wine: Steuben Blush

Steuben Blush

CALVARESI WINERY
Pennsylvania Table Wine
Produced and Bottled By
CALVARESI WINERY
Bernville, PA

Hours

Thursday–Friday, 1:00 P.M. to 6:00 P.M.; Saturday–Sunday, noon to 5:00 P.M.

Directions

Calvaresi Winery is located 10 miles northwest of Reading, just off Route 183. Take Route 183 through Bernville. Turn right on Shartlesville Road at the Bernville Elementary School. The winery is ½ mile on the right.

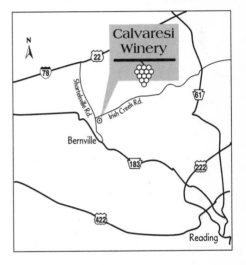

🍇 Chaddsford Winery

632 Baltimore Pike, Chadds Ford, PA 19317
PHONE: (610) 388-6221
FAX: (610) 388-0360
E-MAIL: cfwine@chaddsford.com
WEBSITE: www.chaddsford.com

LOCATION: Southeast, Philadelphia Area
(Chester County Wine Trail)

CHADDSFORD WINERY, IN CHESTER COUNTY WEST OF PHILADELPHIA, IS Pennsylvania's largest winery. In 1998 it produced 73,000 gallons. When the winery opened in 1983, it had 7,000 gallons of wine for sale from the 1982 vintage, making the winery larger when it opened than half of the current wineries in the state of Pennsylvania.

Eric and Lee Miller, the proprietors of Chaddsford, both had backgrounds in the wine industry, Eric as a winemaker and Lee as a writer. Eric spent part of his childhood in Saint-Romain, a small village in the Burgundy region of France. As a young man, he worked with his father, who in 1969 had founded one of the first boutique wineries in New York, Benmarl Vineyards. It was at Benmarl that Eric learned to make wine. Lee had worked in advertising and published *The Pennsylvania Grape Letter and Wine News,* a bimonthly newsletter, as well as several books about wine with Hudson Cattell in the late 1970s.

In 1980 Eric and Lee left Benmarl for western New York State and Chadwick Bay Wine Company. They soon began planning a winery of their own in an area that reminded Eric more of the Burgundy region where he had grown up—southeastern Pennsylvania. They found an investor to help make their plans a reality and a location along a major highway with a 200-year-old house they could live in and a barn for the winery facility. In 1982 they moved to Chadds Ford, Pennsylvania.

Because Chaddsford Winery is located close to Philadelphia, Wilmington, and Baltimore, it draws many of its customers from those areas, as well as southern New Jersey. In the summertime, many of the people stopping by the winery are tourists; the rest of the year, their customers are more locally based. The Millers market their wine at the winery, at one permanent extension near New Hope, in the State Stores run by the Pennsylvania Liquor Control Board, in many restaurants, and through distributors in states from Massachusetts to Virginia.

The Millers have always held many special events, including a variety of festivals and special dinners. Winery activities swing into high gear in early April, and most major events finish by Labor Day weekend. (They have found that it is better not to hold big festivals during the grape harvest.) In 1999 they featured a Friday night concert series with various types of music including blues, jazz, folk, and Cajun. The weekend of July 4th is the winery's Sangria Fest, which includes wine tastings, live bands, and Sangria sampling.

Eric and Lee have worked hard to make sure that everyone on the winery's staff is knowledgeable about wine, not just from Chaddsford, but from other regions of the world as well. Both at the many wine and food events and in the tasting room, the winery stresses the importance of matching styles of wine with food.

At Chaddsford Winery, Eric Miller uses a wine thief to extract some wine for tasting from one of his barrels.

For the first six years, Chaddsford Winery did not have its own vineyards. The Millers bought all their fruit from vineyards in Erie County and the southeastern part of Pennsylvania. In 1989 the Millers purchased an existing vineyard of about 15 acres in northern Chester County and later added another 15 acres. Over the course of ten years, Eric has removed the Chancellor and added more Chardonnay, Chambourcin, and Pinot Noir. Other varietals that have been planted include Barbera, Petite Verdot, and Cabernet Franc.

Rather than add more acres to their own vineyard, Eric has been encouraging other people in Chester County to plant grapes. He looks for people who will put in those varieties that he wants and who will follow his suggestions in the vineyard. These growers planted between 15 and 20 acres in 1999, and more acres are scheduled for planting in 2000.

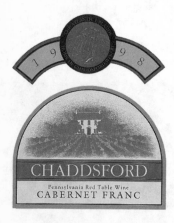

Wine List

Dry: Chardonnay, Proprietors Reserve White (Seyval, Vidal, and Vignoles), Pinot Grigio, Viognier, Proprietors Reserve Red (Chambourcin), Chambourcin, Cabernet Franc, Cabernet Sauvignon, Merican (Cabernet Sauvignon, Cabernet Franc, and Merlot), Pinot Noir, Dolcetto

Semisweet: Riesling, Chaddsford Blush (Steuben)

Sweet: Niagara, Dessert Riesling

Seasonal Wines: Spring Wine (Riesling, Vignoles, Seyval, and Vidal), Spiced Apple, Holiday Spirit

Best-selling Wines: Chaddsford Blush, Apple, Spring Wine, Chardonnay

Hours

Daily, noon–6:00 P.M. (Closed Mondays from January 1 to April 1.)

Services and Events

Outdoor concerts, festivals, wine education classes, special tastings, private labels, wine baskets, bocce court.

Directions

The winery is located on Route 1 west of Philadelphia, between the Brandywine River Museum and Longwood Gardens. From Philadelphia, take I-95 south to Route 322 West. Take Route 322 West to Route 1, turn left, and go 6 miles. The winery is on the left.

Extensions

The Chaddsford Wine Shop and Tasting Room, Shop #20, Route 263, Peddler's Village, Lahaska, (215) 794-9655, e-mail: cfwbucks @voicenet.com. Four holiday mall stores open before Christmas.

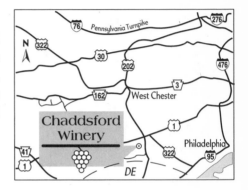

🍇 Cherry Valley Vineyards

R.D. 5, Box 5100, Saylorsburg, PA 18353
PHONE: (570) 992-2255
FAX: (570) 992-5083
E-MAIL: cvwine@epix.net
WEBSITE: www.cherryvalleyvineyard.com

LOCATION: **Mountains, Northeast Area
(Lehigh Valley Wine Trail)**

IN THE 1970S DOMINIC AND MARY SORRENTI WERE IN THE RESTAURANT and food business in Delaware Water Gap. Mary's father was concerned that their business endeavors didn't give them enough time with family, however, and he urged Mary to buy a farm and start a winery as a family project. The Sorrentis bought their farm in 1980, planted the first grapes in 1983, and opened the winery in 1986 with 1,200 gallons of wine for sale.

Today, almost twenty years later, Mary's father's dream has come true. Cherry Valley Vineyards is a thriving family business, with a 15-acre vineyard and a winery that produces 19,000 gallons. And perhaps best of all, the second generation is beginning to take over the management of the winery, although Mary and Dominic are still very much involved.

Dominic taught their son Nick everything he knew about making wine, and he and Mary sent Nick to Burgundy to refine his winemaking skills. Now Nick is making the wines and Dominic has become winemaker "emeritus," a status that allows him to taste and help with blends (the more romantic aspects of making wine) while Nick presses grapes, racks wine, moves barrels, and does the other labor-intensive parts of the winemaking process. Mary manages the business end of the winery and runs the tasting room with the help of their daughters Lucia, who is still in school, and Elysia, who does the bookkeeping and handles the private labeling. Another son, Sonny, helps in the vineyard when he has the time on weekends. In the interim, Jeremy Pattison is the vineyard manager while also attending East Stroudsburg University.

Because the second generation is coming into the family business, the Sorrentis have changed and enhanced their plans for the growth of the winery. In the spring of 1999 they planted 6,000 vines of Cabernet Franc, Cabernet Sauvignon, Chambourcin, and Foch. They want to have a total of 25 acres of producing vines in four years and plan to increase the size of the winery to 25,000 gallons as more of their vines come into production. More wine production will probably lead to another winery expansion, such as adding a separate building for bottle

A "monk," played by local actor Bill Keller, is the tour guide on weekends at Cherry Valley Vineyards.

and case storage and perhaps a "cave" for barrel storage so that the red wines can be held for a longer period of time.

Its location gives Cherry Valley Vineyards two advantages: It's easy to get to from a major highway, and the property is adjacent to Pennsylvania state game lands and the mountain ridge with the Appalachian Trail. The Sorrentis have used both to help sell their wine. Large billboards announce the presence of the winery to passing traffic, and over the years these signs have succeeded in drawing many customers. More recently, Mary came up with an idea to make use of the Appalachian Trail location: The winery now hosts guided Appalachian hike and wine tours. The participants meet at the winery on a Sunday morning, are shuttled up to the trailhead near Wind Gap, hike back to the winery in about three hours, and then are given a hot lunch buffet and a tour of the winery. Originally the hikes were held once a month, and Mary's goal was to have about forty people on each hike. By 1998, however, every hike was filled to capacity, with the numbers of people growing to more than sixty. In 1999 more than twenty hikes were scheduled between mid-April and November, and the Sorrentis have added both a kitchen and a pavilion to handle the crowds.

Wine List

Dry: Chablis (Vidal, Seyval, and Cayuga), Cayuga White, Burgundy (Léon Millot, Foch, and Baco Noir), Foch, Baco Noir, Léon Millot, DeChaunac, Chardonnay, Riesling

Semidry: Seyval Blanc, Kittatinny Red (75 percent Léon Millot, Foch, and Baco Noir; 25 percent Concord)

Semisweet: Cherry Valley Blush (Seyval, Vidal, Cayuga, and Steuben), Niagara, Pink Catawba, Ravat, Riesling

Sweet: Cherry Valley Pink (Concord and Niagara), Concord

Fruit Wines: Apple, Peach, Plum, Raspberry, Blueberry, Strawberry, Cherry

Sparkling: Classic Champagne (75 percent Chardonnay), Blush Spumante (blend of Seyval, Vidal, Cayuga, Steuben, and Catawba), Niagara Spumante, and seven other fruit Spumantes

Best-selling Wines: Dry reds and Spumante wines

Hours

Daily, 11:00 A.M. to 5:00 P.M. Tours on weekends, 1:00 to 5:00 P.M.

Services and Events

Personalized labeling, custom gift baskets, Appalachian hikes and hayrides, picnic pavilion with seating for a hundred people for weddings, parties, meetings, and music events (catering available).

Directions

The winery is just off Route 33 between the Allentown-Bethlehem-Easton area and Stroudsburg. Take the Saylorsburg exit; turn left (south) onto Route 115. In about ³/4 mile, turn left on Lower Cherry Valley Road. The road takes you under Route 33; the winery is immediately on the right.

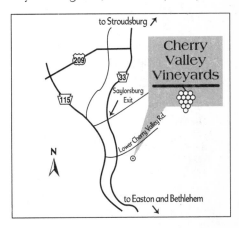

🍇 Christian W. Klay Winery

412 Fayette Springs Rd., Chalk Hill, PA 15421
PHONE: (724) 439-3424
FAX: (724) 439-1553
WEBSITE: www.hhs.net/cwklay

LOCATION: **Mountains, Southwest Area**

THE CHRISTIAN W. KLAY WINERY BEGAN AS THE DREAM OF SURGEON John Klay, who wanted to have a vineyard where he could do some research on grape varieties and also make some wine. He read widely on all aspects of growing and making wine, and when he went into practice in Pittsburgh, he and his wife, Sharon, began to look for the perfect farm for a vineyard and winery. The search took three years. When they found the farm in Chalk Hill 60 miles southeast of Pittsburgh, John liked the soils and Sharon saw the potential of the barn.

John ordered one thousand vines of more than one hundred different varietals for planting in 1989. As Sharon tells the story, in the spring the vines arrived, but John didn't. His surgical practice in Pittsburgh was growing, so Sharon planted the vines and quickly realized she needed to know more about growing grapes and making wine. By 1990 she had teamed up with Ray Matthews, the father of a young girl Sharon had first hired to hoe weeds around the young vines. Ray is a detail person who had worked in quality control for Volkswagen and was intrigued with the idea of establishing a vineyard. With John's backing, Sharon and Ray set out to learn how to grow grapes and make wine. Over the next few years, they visited some two hundred wineries from Tennessee to Ontario. They attended conferences, asked questions, and sought out knowledge-able people, learning as they went.

From the original vineyard of one thousand vines, the Klays' vineyard has now expanded to include about 12 acres, all of it surrounded by 12-foot-high deer fence. There are still many more varieties of grapes than are found in most vineyards—for good reasons. For one, the different kinds of grapes give Sharon more options when she is blending wines. And then too some grape varieties are hardier than others, and it seemed to the Klays that growing many varieties would ensure that some grapes would ripen in their vineyard in spite of cold winter temperatures, spring frosts, and summer heat and humidity.

Ray has learned ways of holding the vines back from bud break in the spring to help prevent damage from spring frosts, and other ways to encourage the grapes to reach their full ripeness. The vines are double pruned. The first pruning removes the bulk of the vegetation; the second pruning takes place after any winter damage or spring frosts have occurred. In the fall, Ray hills up dirt around all the vines and plants a cover crop of vetch or rye both to hold the soil and to compete with and slow down the growth of the vines in the springtime. In the summer, the row middles are clean-tilled, which allows the many rocks in the soil to absorb and then reflect back to the vines the heat of the sun. Ray also uses leaf pruning and shoot thinning to help to balance the amount of the grape crop so that the grapes are of high quality—and ripe.

After years of research and eight years in establishing the vineyard, Sharon, John, and Ray produced their first commercial harvest and opened the Christian W. Klay Winery in May 1997. The winery is

The "family" at Christian W. Klay Winery includes (from left to right) Sharon and John Klay, their son Christian (for whom the winery is named), and Ray Mathews, vineyard manager. Many people who visit the winery will meet Sharon and Ray, but John and Chris are not at the winery as frequently.

named for Sharon and John's son Christian, who was twelve when the winery opened. The entire barn was rebuilt to accommodate the winery. The lower level houses the winery and the tasting room, and the upper level of the barn is one large area in which special events, such as weddings or Saturday afternoon jazz concerts, are held.

Sharon was originally trained as a dental hygienist and later became an artist. Her background in dental hygiene provided the knowledge of chemistry necessary for being a winemaker, and painting influences her in the art of blending. The many different wine varietals that are available from the vineyard serve as her palette; through her art of blending, they are crafted into the final work of art—a bottle of wine. Sharon recognizes that many of the finest wines in the world are not made from a single variety of grapes, but are artful blends. Skilled winemakers take advantage of the individual nuances of different varietals to create a blended wine that is better than any of its components.

The winery is located just off the National Road, near Fort Necessity and not far from Fallingwater, the house designed by Frank Lloyd Wright, so more than 1.5 million people pass through the area every year. Sharon hopes to draw those people into the winery, while also encouraging local people to view it as "their" regional winery. She knows she is selling not just wine, but the romance of wine and the special location of the winery. She calls her wines the National Road Collection, and each is named for a local historic site. Once a month from May to October, Sharon holds wine and dine dinners in the woods near the vineyard. The guests are taken by haywagon out past the vineyards to a clearing in the woods, where they are served a gourmet dinner featuring Sharon's wines.

Wine List

Dry: Blanc de Lafayette (primarily Vidal, with Muscat Ottonel to add a floral component), Fort Necessity (Chardonnay), Jumonville Glen Red (Rosette, St. Croix, and a little Chambourcin), Stone House Red (Cabernet Sauvignon and Lemberger)

Semidry: Nemacolin Castle (primarily Seyval with some Vignoles and Edelweiss), Washington Tavern White (Cayuga), Washington Tavern Red (Léon Millot, Baco Noir, and some Chambourcin and Foch)

Semisweet: Searight's Tollhouse (Aurore and Gewürztraminer), White Swan Tavern (Vignoles), Chestnut Ridge Sunset (blend of French-American hybrids), Spiced Apple

Best-selling Wines: Washington Tavern Red, Chestnut Ridge Sunset (a White Zinfandel–style wine)

Hours

Sunday–Thursday, noon to 6:00 P.M.; Friday–Saturday, 11:00 A.M. to 7:00 P.M.

Services and Events

Gift baskets, personalized labels, large barn area for social events such as weddings or family reunions.

Directions

The winery is located approximately 60 miles southeast of Pittsburgh. From Route 40 in Chalk Hill, turn south onto Fayette Springs Road at the Christmas shop opposite the post office. The winery is 300 yards on the left.

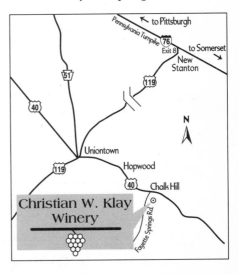

Clover Hill Vineyards & Winery

9850 Newtown Rd., Breinigsville, PA 18031
PHONE: (610) 395-2468
FAX: (610) 366-1246
E-MAIL: clover01@fast.net
WEBSITE: www.cloverhillwinery.com

LOCATION: Southeast, Lehigh Valley
(Lehigh Valley Wine Trail)

JOHN AND PAT SKRIP ORIGINALLY PLANNED TO PLANT THEIR FARM WITH Christmas trees. John had started a contracting business with his brother, however, and somehow the trees didn't get planted. One day, after he had been in the contracting business for four years without a vacation, he went home and announced to Pat that they were going to Florida the next day. Pat agreed, and the following day they were on an Eastern Airlines flight headed toward Florida. During the flight, John picked up an in-flight magazine and found an article about growing grapes in the eastern United States, complete with a picture of grapes covered with ice to protect them from a spring frost. He handed the article to Pat and said, "Here's what we ought to be growing!"

The first grapes were planted at Clover Hill Vineyards in 1975, not long after that trip to Florida. The winery, however, did not open until 1985, when the hobby finally turned into a real venture. Clover Hill opened with 2,700 gallons for sale; by 1998 production had increased to 45,000 gallons. The original vineyard around the winery has a total of 6 acres planted, and in 1986 the Skrips added a second vineyard of 25 acres in Robesonia that they call the Heidelberg Vineyard. Two other vineyards have been planted nearer to the winery: the Sunrise Vineyard, a 10-acre parcel east of the winery on Newtown Road, and the Sunset Vineyard, just south of Route 222 about 1/2 mile from the winery. As of spring 1999 a total of 55 acres was planted with vines.

Other changes have come to the winery over the years. In 1987 John sold his part of the contracting business and concentrated on the winery full-time. The Skrips' three children grew up and went to college, and two of them have returned to work at the winery. John III studied at Fresno State University after graduating from the Pennsylvania State University and now is the winemaker for Clover Hill. The Skrips' youngest, Kari, graduated from Frostburg State University in 1999 and is helping Pat with the business and marketing end of the winery. She is planning to study in Australia in 2000 to gain more experience to ultimately help expand the family business.

When the winery first opened in 1985, all the winemaking processes, bottle and case storage, and wine sales took place in a well-insulated building on the hill above the vineyard. It wasn't long, however, before John felt as if he were working inside a submarine, as the spaces became tighter and tighter with more tanks and equipment. As a result, the Skrips constructed a new building just for making wine at the bottom of the hill, retaining only the tasting room and wine sales in the old facility. Since then the new winery building has had three additions, most recently a

Many different pieces of vineyard equipment, including the mechanical harvester, were lined up outside the winery building at Clover Hill Vineyards & Winery before one of the winery's festivals.

new bottling room in late 1997. The Skrips plan to convert the end of the building, where agricultural equipment has been stored, into a new barrel room and to add a new tasting room so that all the functions of the winery will be based at the bottom of the hill.

Wine List

Dry: Rayon d'Or, Oak Vidal, Clover Hill Red (proprietary blend), Chambourcin, Cabernet Sauvignon

Semidry: Vidal Blanc, Turtle Rock Red (Chambourcin)

Semisweet: Cayuga White, Riesling, DeChaunac Rosé, DeChaunac

Sweet: Vignoles, Niagara, Catawba, Alden, Clover Hill Rosé (Vidal Blanc, Vignoles, and Chambourcin), Concord, Spiced Apple, Raspberry, Holiday Rosé

Sparkling: Brut Sparkling Wine (Seyval Blanc and Rayon d'Or), Clover Hill Cuvée (proprietary blend)

Best-selling Wines: Varies from location to location: Dry reds sell well at the Allentown Farmers Market, while sweeter wines do better in Robesonia.

Hours

Monday–Saturday, 11:00 A.M. to 5:00 P.M.; Sunday, noon to 5:00 P.M.; Christmas holiday hours: Monday–Saturday, 9:00 A.M. to 6:00 P.M.; Sunday, noon to 5:00 P.M.

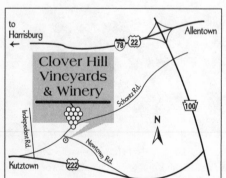

Services and Events

Custom labeling, baskets, wine racks.

Directions

The winery is west of Allentown. Take Route 78/22 to the exit for

Route 100 South. Go south on Route 100 to the second traffic light, and turn right onto Schantz Road. Go 3 miles, and turn left on Newtown Road. The winery entrance is on the right.

Extensions

- R.D. #1, Box 299, West Meadow Rd., Robesonia, (610) 693-8383 (same hours as winery).
- Allentown Fairgrounds Farmers' Market, 17th and Chew Streets, Allentown, (610) 439-3969 (open Thursday, 9:00 A.M. to 8:00 P.M.; Friday, 8:00 A.M. to 8:00 P.M.; Saturday, 8:00 A.M. to 6:00 P.M.).
- Berkshire Mall, 1665 State Hill Rd., Wyomissing, (610) 655-9870 (open mall hours).
- Lehigh Valley Mall (seasonal location), Route 22 and MacArthur Rd., Whitehall, (610) 266-6016.
- Coventry Mall (seasonal location), Routes 724 and 100, Pottstown, (610) 326-1491 (open mall hours).

Conneaut Cellars Winery

P.O. Box 5075, 12005 Conneaut Lake Road, Conneaut Lake, PA 16316
PHONE: (814) 382-3999
TOLL-FREE: (877) CCW-WINE (229-9463)
FAX: (814) 382-6151
WEBSITE: www.ccw-wine.com

LOCATION: Lake Erie

"WE'RE NOT A FRENCH WINERY OR A GERMAN WINERY; WE'RE AN AMERICAN winery, and I want it to be a part of this state, so that it looks like it belongs in the Lake Erie region of Pennsylvania. We represent the area, the region, and that's what makes us unique. We're not trying to compete with Gallo or to be a soda pop factory. We try to sell an experience, and to offer local people wines they like to drink." These words summarize the approach of Joal Wolf, second-generation owner of Conneaut Cellars Winery in Conneaut Lake, Pennsylvania.

The winery was started in 1982 by Joal's parents, Alan and Phyllis Wolf, as a third career for Alan, whose first career had been in the military and second in education. While in Germany with the State Department in the 1950s, Alan first became interested in wine. When he began his teaching career in the late 1950s, he also started to make wine, since his salary was not large enough to allow him to buy wine on a regular basis. He and Phyllis were active in helping to get the initial legislation passed to allow farm wineries in Pennsylvania, and after the Limited Act passed in 1968, they considered opening a winery. The Wolfs were turned down for a loan, however, because the bank didn't think Alan would be able to obtain the grapes to make wine, and he wasn't interested in starting a vineyard. It was not until Alan retired from education in 1981 that wine-making became a full-time career.

Alan and Phyllis's son Joal started to help make wine with his parents when he was two years old. After graduating from Penn State with a degree in finance, Joal served in Europe with the U.S. Army for four years. He returned to the winery in 1988 and assisted his father in making the wine and in all other areas of the business. By 1993 Joal had earned an MBA and was working full-time as winemaster at Conneaut

Cellars Winery. The family had planned for an orderly transition to allow Joal to take over the winery in three or four years, but these plans had to be accelerated when Alan passed away suddenly in February 1995. Joal bought the winery from his mother in 1996, but Phyllis remains active in the winery as marketing director.

Alan had established the winery with an eye toward what would happen in the future. "Dad was always on the cutting edge," Joal notes. "He was creative and willing to try new ways of doing things. He was one of the first to use steam cleaning in an eastern winery, and he developed intricate spreadsheets on the computer for handling the winery's financial records." Joal sees himself as more willing to wait, but he too is a planner. Since he took over the winery, he put on an addition that doubles the amount of space and recently redesigned the wine labels. He has plans to improve the equipment used in making the wine, to add a pole barn to house a tool shop and bottle storage, and to put a roof over the crush pad. And he has already put in the necessary electricity and drains for future expansion.

But Joal does not plan for the winery to become big. He thinks 10,000 cases is a good size that will allow him to serve his local customer base—people from the local area and those who come to visit the lake—without losing sight of the fact that Conneaut Cellars is a part of the region.

As wineries grow larger, they often need more space and a wider range in tank sizes. At Conneaut Cellars Winery, Joal Wolf doubled the size of the winery facility to provide more space both for winemaking and for storage of wine in these tanks.

Conneaut Cellars Winery does not grow any of its own grapes. Most of the fruit that the winery uses is grown in Erie County, about 35 miles north and east of Conneaut Lake.

Wine List

Dry: Vidal Blanc, Chardonnay, Merlot, Cabernet Sauvignon, Cabernet Franc

Off-dry: Gewürztraminer, Reflections (Chardonnay and Riesling), Seyval, Snug Harbor (Vidal Blanc), Sadsbury Red (Chancellor), Finn Ditch Red (Chambourcin)

Semidry: Wolf Island (Delaware), Riesling, Midway Blush, Colonel Crawford (Léon Millot), Ice House Misty Bubbly Wine

Semisweet: Princess Snowater (Catawba), Allegheny Gold (Vignoles), Pymatuning Rose (Pink Catawba), Summit Red (DeChaunac), Ice House Misty Bubbly Pink

Sweet: Huidekoper (Niagara), Hazel Park Red (Concord)

Best-selling Wines: Hazel Park Red (sweet Concord) and Princess Snowater (Catawba)

Hours

Daily, 10:00 A.M. to 6:00 P.M. (except January 1, Easter, Thanksgiving, and Christmas).

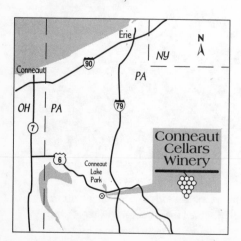

Directions

From the Pennsylvania Turnpike, take exit 3 for Cranberry and then I-79 north toward Erie. Take exit 36B, and go west on Route 322 and U.S. Route 6. Go 6 miles; the winery is on the left just before town.

Country Creek Winery

133 Cressman Rd., Telford, PA 18969
PHONE: (215) 723-6516

LOCATION: **Southeast, Philadelphia Area**

COUNTRY CREEK WINERY IS ONE OF THE OLDER WINERIES IN PENNSYLVANIA. It first opened in 1978 as a partnership between Bill Scheidell, who owned Appleville Orchards and was the winery's business manager, and Fred Klee, who served as winemaker. Though the two had big plans for expanding the winery and adding a vineyard, they never achieved the success they desired. After a serious partnership dispute, the two sold the winery to a former professional football player and a former professional basketball player. But though the second owners may have been successful in the sports arena, neither was particularly good at running a winery or marketing wine.

In the early 1990s Doug Klein and his wife, Joy, bought 10 acres of land that included the barn where the winery was housed. Doug, as the winery's landlord, was willing to work with the winery owners and help them expand their business. That strategy didn't seem to work, so he offered to buy the winery, and much to his surprise, they accepted his offer.

In 1995 the winery reopened, this time as a partnership between Doug and Joy, and Doug's sister and brother-in-law, Paul and Donna Killian. All four had other jobs outside the wine industry, but they viewed the winery as an enjoyable enterprise for the family to participate in. Their production in 1995 was only 240 gallons, but by 1997 it had increased to 2,000 gallons. In 1998 Paul Killian was killed in a car accident. This event had ramifications for the winery, and as one consequence, Donna, who is the winemaker for the group, made only 600 gallons during that year's harvest.

Today the winery and its owners are on the rebound. Doug, Joy, and Donna are working hard to improve the quality of the wines and rebuild the winery's image. They would like to make some physical changes to the winery, such as adding insulation to the building and improving the

Donna Killian, winemaker and one of the owners at Country Creek Winery, stands in front of the self-service tasting bar.

facilities for holding special events, such as parties and weddings. They feel that the winery provides a lot of fun in their lives, from bottling runs with four small children trying to help out, to listening to Doug's band play in the room next to the tasting area.

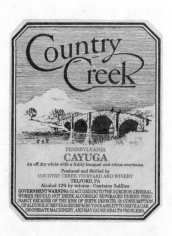

The winery is located in a bank barn that dates back to the late 1800s, with the winemaking area in the bottom part of the barn and the tasting room upstairs. An outside staircase leads up to that area and to the room used for band practices and small parties.

Wine List

Dry: Seyval Blanc, Vidal, DeChaunac, Baco Noir, Chambourcin

Semidry: Cayuga

Sweet: Niagara, Concord

Fruit Wines: Country Apple, Strawberry (in season)

Best-selling Wine: Concord

Hours

Saturday and Sunday, noon to 5:00 P.M.

Services and Events

Room for small parties up to thirty people.

Directions

At the Lansdale exit of the Northeast Extension of the Pennsylvania Turnpike, take Route 63 west through Harleysville. From the intersection with Route 113 in Harleysville, continue west on Route 63 for 2½ miles. Turn right on Longmill Road, then take the next left onto Moyer Road. After you cross the bridge over the Perkiomen Creek, immediately turn right onto Cressman Road. The winery is on the right in less than ½ mile.

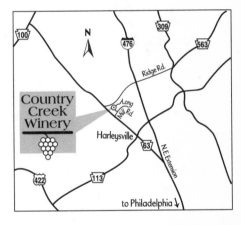

🍇 Evergreen Valley Vineyards

R.R. #1, Box 173D, Evergreen Rd., Luthersburg, PA 15848
PHONE AND FAX: (814) 583-7575
E-MAIL: vintner@evwinery.com
WEBSITE: www.evwinery.com

LOCATION: **Mountains, Northwest Area**

IN 1980 MARK GEARHART PLANTED FIFTY DIFFERENT VARIETIES OF GRAPES at his house outside of Luthersburg in northwestern Pennsylvania. He had no idea what would grow, because there was no history of viticulture in that part of the state. However, he had a southern exposure and was reasonably sure that the climate would allow some grapes to survive and prosper. In the mid-1980s he began to look for a farm. He wanted the right place for growing grapes—the right land, near a road, and with access to city water, phone lines, and electricity.

In many respects, the history of Evergreen Valley Vineyards is Mark's quest to find a site and plant a vineyard capable of growing quality wine grapes, and to build a winery designed for making good wine. Mark has achieved his goal on both accounts. The vineyard is now producing, and the quality of the grapes is reflected in the wines that Mark is making. The wines at Evergreen, as well as the unique story, make a visit to the winery worth the trip.

Mark encountered numerous problems in trying to find suitable land in the coal country of northwestern Pennsylvania. Much of the land was forested and could take as long as ten to fifteen years to turn into vineyard, other land had been strip-mined for coal, and the farmland that was in production often was owned by a farmer who either didn't want to sell or wanted to sell at high prices to coal companies. Gradually it became apparent to Mark that the best type of land to look for would be property that had already been strip-mined, but where the soil had been piled up during the stripping process and then mixed as it was returned to cover the stripped area. It also was important to find land that was out of bond (a legal aspect of coal mining) and that had the right aspect or topographic orientation. It took four years for Mark to find a place that met all his criteria. The 64-acre farm was located not far from his house, and the land sloped from a ridge down into a valley to the south.

As a vineyard location, the farm has proved to be a good site. The temperatures there are consistently higher by about 8 degrees than in the town of DuBois, about 5 miles away, and because the warm air rises up the valley toward the ridge, there is a constant breeze blowing.

Mark and his parents purchased the property in 1990, and the first grapes were planted in 1992. At that point, Mark began to plan the construction of the winery. Water and a phone line were no problem, but the power company estimated that it would cost at least $25,000 to run electricity to the winery site, with monthly charges added on after the initial installation. Mark was an engineer by training, and decided that he could supply his own power at a much lower cost.

His first power source was a car battery that he used to run his answering machine. That, however, began to be a drain on his gas tank, as he had to run his jeep to recharge the battery. Next he added a solar component, installing a 40-watt solar panel that could be adjusted according to the seasons and the angle of the sun. Solar panels become useless when the weather is gray and cloudy, as it inevitably is in northwestern Pennsylvania in November—one of the peak times when power is needed in a winery facility, after the grapes are harvested and the winemaking process has begun.

Mark's next move was to add a windmill. His version is a high-tech model that is located about 3 feet above the roof of the winery. It takes advantage of the constant breeze that comes up the valley, over the vineyard, to the winery building, and it produces 388 watts. As backup, the winery also has a propane tank that provides fuel for gas lamps and a gas refrigerator. Two more solar panels were added,

Evergreen Valley Vineyards uses three sources of power in their vineyards and winery: solar, wind, and propane. Here Mark Gearhart checks a solar panel that collects energy to run the electric deer fence that surrounds the vineyard.

one to provide power for the small building that houses the winery's bathroom, and one to supply power to the electric deer fence that surrounds the entire vineyard.

Evergreen Valley Vineyards opened in 1997 as the state's, and perhaps the nation's, only winery that supplies all its own energy needs. In 1998 Mark produced 1,800 gallons of wine, and in the next few years he would like to increase production to about 5,000 gallons, while remaining dependent on the wind and the sun for all his electricity.

Wine List

Dry: Chardonnay, Seyval Blanc, DeChaunac, Baco Noir, Léon Millot, Maréchal Foch, Chancellor, Rosette

Semidry: Catawba, Cayuga, Estate Cayuga, Aurore

Sweet: Steuben, Fredonia

Best-selling Wines: Baco Noir, Fredonia

Hours

Wednesday–Sunday, 10:00 A.M. to 6:00 P.M.

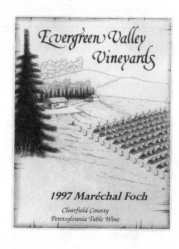

1997 Maréchal Foch
Clearfield County
Pennsylvania Table Wine

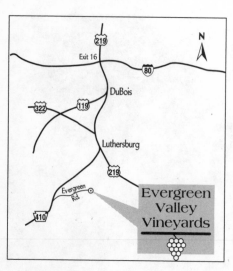

Directions

From I-80, take exit 16 for Route 219 and go south through DuBois to the intersection with Route 410. Turn right at the sign onto Route 410, and go west 2 miles. Turn sharply left onto Evergreen Road. Go straight for 0.7 miles; the winery will be on the right.

🍇 Fox Ridge Vineyard and Winery

3528 E. Market St., York, PA 17402
PHONE: (717) 755-3384
FAX: (717) 755-1248

LOCATION: **Southeast, Susquehanna Valley**

To get to Harold Neibert's winery, Fox Ridge Vineyard and Winery, the visitor has to go through the first floor of his animal hospital in York, Pennsylvania, past the talking parrot, past the closed doors with barking dogs requesting attention, down a corridor, and into the basement. It looks like an ordinary basement, except that it is packed with small-scale winemaking equipment. There are a few oak barrels, but for the most part, the wines are all in 5-gallon glass bottles called carboys—rows and rows of them. As Harold opens more doors, there are additional rooms with more rows of carboys, in all shades of the winemaking rainbow, from deep inky purple to pale reds to amber and light yellow.

Harold opened his veterinary hospital in 1952 and began making wine as an amateur in 1974. When he planted his first grapes in 1983, he already had a wall full of ribbons he had won as an amateur winemaker, both in American Wine Society competitions and at the York County Fair. When he received his commercial license in 1994, he just continued to make wine the same way he always has—in small batches using carboys. If a carboy is not quite full, rather than top it up with some other wine, Harold adds marbles. The marbles raise the level of the wine to fill the carboy; when the wine is taken out of the carboy, the marbles are easy to retrieve, wash, and reuse.

Fox Ridge wines are not sold from this cellar. A few doors down from the vet hospital, in a small shopping center on a busy street east of York, is the Spielgrund Wine Shop, a wine and beer supply shop that has been run by Harold's wife, Shirley, for the past ten years. When the wine shop first opened ten years ago, it sold wine- and beermaking supplies and equipment, and also served as an outlet for Allegro Vineyards. Before Shirley and Harold opened their own winery, she also sold wines for Chaddsford Winery and Hunters Valley Winery. When they opened the

Harold Neibert in the vineyard at Fox Ridge Vineyard and Winery.

winery in 1994, they added their wine to the product mix sold in the shop. Today only Fox Ridge wines are for sale there. Shirley handles the business end of running the winery. She takes care of the sales and promotion of the wine, does the winery paperwork, and runs the wine shop, in addition to a woodstove and Amish furniture shop next door.

Harold says his goal is to be the smallest and best winery in Pennsylvania. That quality begins in the vineyard. Harold grows about 1½ acres of many different kinds of grapes high on a ridge east of York. His daughter Cindy, who is also a veterinarian and works with her dad, lives on Fox Ridge Road, and the vineyard is adjacent to her house. According to Harold, he has no plans to add onto the vineyard but occasionally fills in a place if he loses a vine. "I don't want to add extensions or restaurant sales; I'm in it for the fun of it, for relaxation and as an escape from the veterinary business. I used to give a lot of my wine away when I was an amateur. Now that we're commercial, at least I can get compensated somewhat for the wines I like to make!"

Wine List

Dry: Villard, Seyval Blanc (oak aged), White Sapphire (Labrusca blend), Cabernet Sauvignon (oak aged), Fox Ridge Red (Foch,

Cabernet Sauvignon, and other red varietals, oak aged), Ridge Runner Red (Labrusca blend), Rougeon, Merlot

Semidry: Winemakers Delight (Vidal and Cayuga), Yorkshire White (Labrusca blend, oak aged), Chambourcin, Crimson Hills

Semisweet: Bavarian White (Vidal and Villard), Cayuga White, Chardonnay, Diamond, Dutchess, Riesling, Seyval Blanc, Smoky White (Labrusca blend, oak aged), Vidal, Chardonel, Melody, Foxes Picnic (Vidal and Rougeon), Catawba, Ramblin Rosé (Labrusca blend plus some Chambourcin, oak aged), Yorktowne Rosé (Labrusca blend plus some Chambourcin), Fireside Spice (Apple with spices), Springetts Red (Labrusca blend), Concord

Sweet: Niagara, Delaware, White Nectar (Labrusca blend plus peach), Maiden's Blush (Catawba and Steuben)

Fruit Wines: Apricot, Blueberry, Peach, Pear, Plum, Raspberry, Strawberry

Best-selling Wines: Niagara, Chardonel

Hours

Tuesday–Friday, 10:00 A.M. to 6:00 P.M.; Saturday, 10:00 A.M. to 4:00 P.M.; Sunday, 1:00 to 4:00 P.M.

Directions

From York, go east on Route 462. From Route 30, take the Mt. Zion Road exit east of York, and go south on Mt. Zion Road. Turn left on Route 462 east. Fox Ridge Vineyard and Winery is on the right in about 1/2 mile, next to the grocery outlet and across from the Volkswagen dealership.

Franklin Hill Vineyards

7833 Franklin Hill Rd., Bangor, PA 18013
PHONE: (610) 588-8708 or (888) 887-2839
FAX: (610) 588-8158
E-MAIL: vineyard@epix.net

LOCATION: Southeast, Lehigh Valley
(Lehigh Valley Wine Trail)

FOR MORE THAN TWELVE YEARS, FRANKLIN HILL VINEYARDS HAS HAD THE distinction of being one of the few wineries in the country to be solely owned by a woman—Elaine Austen. In addition, most of the other roles at the winery are also filled by women: The winemaker is Bonnie Pysher, the vineyard manager is Linda Fleming, and marketing and sales are managed by Jennifer Fleischer, Elaine's daughter. Elaine is quick to recognize that the winery has always had some male help. Her father, Walter Pivinski, has helped her run one of the winery's extensions, and recently her son, Adam Flatt, has taken over much of the farm management while helping run the extension in Bethlehem.

Elaine did not set out to have a business run by women. In the 1970s she and her first husband, Charles Flatt, were what Elaine describes as "back-to-the-land hippies." While living in New Jersey, they discovered the Delaware River Valley and the small town of Bangor. They began to look for property in that area, and in 1975 they found a 35-acre farm outside Bangor, complete with a three-room house that was marginally large enough for a family of four. It was the fulfillment of Elaine's dream since Woodstock—to return to the land and become as self-sufficient as possible. The following year the first acre of Foch was planted, and in subsequent years Elaine planted more vines: 2 acres of Seyval and DeChaunac, 3 acres of Cayuga White, and 6 acres of Vidal. Today the vineyard has a total of 13 acres.

The winery was opened in 1982, the same year that Bonnie started to help Charles make the wine. One major problem was the fact that the farm was landlocked. It had no direct access to the local road, and it took several years to resolve the dispute with neighbors over property lines and driveway access. As a result, the winery has had at least one extension since 1984, when Elaine's dad began to run one winery store in Stroudsburg.

In 1986 Charles left Elaine and the winery. Initially Elaine was not sure that she and Bonnie could handle the vineyard and the winery themselves. She decided to give it a try, however, since she loved the land, the lifestyle, and the industry—and at that point, it was all she had. She and Bonnie sought the advice of winemaker friends nearby, such as Sid Butler at Slate Quarry Winery and Jerry Forest at Buckingham Valley, and gradually built up their winemaking knowledge. Winning a gold medal for one of their wines also gave Elaine additional confidence that Franklin Hill Vineyards could not only survive, but grow and thrive.

As the winery grew, the need for additional help also increased. Elaine added other women who live along Franklin Hill Road to the staff. After the school bus left in the morning, they would come and work for Elaine while their children were in school. Because of Elaine's commitment to the idea of putting children first, Franklin Hill Vineyards is known today as a model workplace for women with children. Her own children grew up and went to college, and ultimately both came back to work with Elaine in the family business. Recently the family expanded with yet another male member, as Elaine married one of her "lovely wine customers," Bob Austen, who lived just down the road from the winery. During the week, Bob has his own job in corporate America, but on weekends he helps Elaine with different wine events, such as pouring wine at a local festival.

What does the future hold for Franklin Hill? It remains to be seen how involved the second generation will be, and their involvement is the key to when and how the winery will grow. In the meantime, Elaine says, "Life is good; I just don't have enough time to be out in the vineyard as much as I'd like!"

Elaine Austen pours samples of her wines from Franklin Hill Vineyards every fall at the Balloon Festival at Shawnee on the Delaware.

The tasting rooms in Franklin Hill's extensions are some of the most attractive in Pennsylvania. This is partly the result of a commitment on the part of Elaine and Jennifer to find interesting, attractive, useful, and fun products to sell in addition to the wine. Also, one of the women who works part-time for Elaine, Ginny Guth, serves as an in-house designer, setting up the displays and creating the wine baskets.

Franklin Hill Vineyards

Northampton County

Chambourcin

Pennsylvania Red Table Wine
Vintage 1998

Produced and Bottled by Franklin Hill Vineyards
Bangor, Pennsylvania
CONTAINS SULFITES

Wine List

Dry: Chardonnay, Seyval Blanc, Seyval Blanc Reserve, Chardonel, Cabernet Franc, Chambourcin, DeChaunac, DeChaunac Reserve, Wedding Reserve Sparkling Wine (Cayuga)

Semidry: Cayuga White, Vidal Blanc, Simply Red (Foch), Country Kiss (mostly Cayuga, plus some Vidal and Foch)

Semisweet: Vignoles, Country Rosé (Cayuga and Vidal in equal parts, plus Foch), Country Apple

Sweet: Country White (Vidal and Cayuga), Niagara, White Sangria (primarily Niagara), Vignoles Reserve, Country Red (Concord)

Best-selling Wine: Country Red

Hours

Monday–Saturday, noon to 5:00 P.M.

Services and Events

Personalized labels, gift baskets, special gift items, such as glasses, wine racks, wine accessories, and gourmet foods.

Directions

From Allentown: Take Route 22 east toward New Jersey to the exit for Route 611 (the last exit in Pennsylvania). Go north on Route 611 to Martins Creek; at the light, turn left onto Front Street. At the top of the hill, turn right onto Franklin Hill Road. Go 1.7 miles, then turn right onto the private winery road. Watch out for the speed bump by the neighboring farmhouse; follow the lane to the left. The winery is at the end of the lane in about 3/4 mile.

From Route 33: Take the exit for Bangor and Route 191. Go east toward Bangor for approximately 5 miles. Watch for Pinocchio's Restaurant on the right. Go down the hill; the next road to the right is Franklin Hill Road. Turn right; the winery lane is on the left in about 2½ miles.

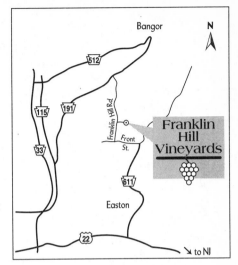

Extensions

- The Wine Shop, Fountain Springs West, Suite 1, Route 611, Tannersville (next to Friendly's).
- The Grape Spot, 36-06 Nicholas St., Easton, (610) 559-7887 (open Wednesday–Saturday, 10:00 A.M. to 5:00 P.M.).
- The Grape Arbor, 597 Main St., Bethlehem, (610) 332-WINE (open Monday–Wednesday, 10:30 A.M. to 6:00 P.M.; Thursday–Saturday, 10:30 A.M. to 8:00 P.M.; Sunday, noon to 5:00 P.M.).

🍇 French Creek Ridge Vineyards

200 Grove Rd., Elverson, PA 19520
PHONE: (610) 286-7754
FAX: (610) 286-7772

LOCATION: Southeast, Philadelphia Area
(Chester County Wine Trail)

WHEN FRED AND JANET MAKI FIRST ACQUIRED THE PROPERTY THAT WAS TO become French Creek Ridge Vineyards, it had a dilapidated barn and a house whose kitchen had no floor. Both buildings dated to approximately 1830, and both definitely had potential. Now, after many years of hard work, the house has been carefully and charmingly restored, and the barn has been converted into a winery with whitewashed walls and drains to make winemaking and cleanup easier. A large brick patio was added to the front of the barn, both to make an attractive entrance and to serve as a location for special winery tastings. The Makis are not finished, however. They plan to change the location of the tasting room to the other end of the barn, where it will be in a separate room with more space.

They began planting the vineyards in 1991 and opened the winery in November 1994. Fred now works full-time at the winery and does all the vineyard work. Janet is officially the winemaker, but with a full-time job outside the winery, she delegates the day-to-day winery work to Fred. The 6 acres of vineyard are planted with Chardonnay, Gewürztraminer, Vidal, Pinot Noir, Cabernet Sauvignon, Cabernet Franc, and a new planting of Viognier, which produced fruit for the first time for the harvest in 1999. The Makis have room to plant possibly another 1 to 1 1/2 acres, but they already can see that that may not be enough space if the winery is to grow to the point where Janet can retire and work full-time at the winery. They are currently talking to friends about planting and growing grapes to meet some of their future grape needs.

The Makis currently produce about 2,500 gallons of Chardonnay, Pinot Noir, Cabernet Sauvignon, Merlot, Vidal Ice Wine, and Champagne. All of the Champagne is produced by the *méthode champenoise* process and is a Blanc de Blanc dry style. In the future, the Makis would like to do more with Champagne in different styles and become known as a premium sparkling wine producer, and they are gradually taking steps to move the winery in that direction.

One small detail has helped increase both their local recognition and sales: After a year of effort, meetings, discussion, letter writing, and more meetings, Janet got approval to put grape logo winery direction signs on Route 23 on either side of Grove Road to let people know that there was a winery in the neighborhood. The "saga of the sign" is a long one, but the outcome was positive, and Janet says that it was definitely worth the effort. It reminds local people to drop in when they have time, and it draws tourists off the highway.

Wine List

Dry: Barrel-fermented Chardonnay, Pinot Noir, Cabernet Sauvignon, Merlot, Blanc de Blanc Champagne (Chardonnay)

The vineyards stretch down the hillside to the vintage-1830 stone barn that houses the winery at French Creek Ridge Vineyards.

Sweet: Vidal Ice Wine

Best-selling Wine: Blanc de Blanc
Champagne

Hours

Thursday–Sunday, 11:00 A.M. to 5:00 P.M.

Services and Events

"Champagne Day" festival.

French Creek Ridge
Vineyards

Chardonnay
1995

P E N N S Y L V A N I A
ALCOHOL 12 % BY VOLUME   750 ML

Directions

French Creek Ridge Vineyards is located relatively close to the Pennsylvania Turnpike. From the west, take exit 22 (east of Reading) off the Turnpike onto Route 23 East. After 6 miles, turn right onto Grove Road. Go up and over the hill, and the winery is on the left. From the east, take exit 23 off the Turnpike, and go north on Route 100 approximately 9 miles. Turn left on Route 23, and travel west about 6 miles. Turn left on Grove Road, go over the hill, and the winery is on the left.

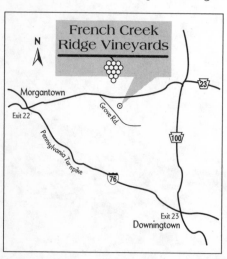

🍇 Galen Glen Vineyard and Winery

Road #1, Box 82-1, Andreas, PA 18211
PHONE: (570) 386-3682
E-MAIL: galenglen@eudoramail.com

LOCATION: **Mountains, Northeast Area**

WHEN SARAH TROXELL WAS WORKING IN PHARMACEUTICAL PACKAGING, she never realized that many of the skills she developed would be so readily transferable to her next job—that of winemaker for the winery started on the family farm with her husband, Galen. The winery, Galen Glen Vineyard and Winery, is one of the newest in Pennsylvania. Though their official opening was held in May 1999, the Troxells opened the winery and began selling wine in September 1998. They own 32 acres, part of a family farm that is more than 150 years old. Galen, who is a mechanical engineer, grew up on the farm, and his goal was always to find a way to move back.

Galen and Sarah built their house high on a hill with beautiful views in every direction. The salesroom is in the basement of the house, the vineyard slopes down the hill, and the winemaking facility is at the bottom of the hill near the house where Galen's parents live. Winery production takes place in what used to be an old potato cellar. Fermenting tanks, tanks for storage, and barrels are in the basement of the building; crushing, bottling, and case storage are all located on the floor above.

The first 2 acres of Chambourcin and Steuben were planted in 1995, and by the spring of 1999 a total of 6½ acres were in the ground. Drawing on his engineering background, Galen and his father developed a special machine to help them plant the vines. As Sarah notes, it helps to have an engineer with a knowledge of welding for jobs both in the vineyard and in the winery. If they need something, Galen can usually fix it or design something to do the job.

Though Galen Glen is farther north than most vineyards that are not protected by a large body of water, it has a relatively high elevation and good air drainage. Galen's family operated a fruit farm there for more

Tractors are multi-function pieces of equipment in a vineyard. After Galen Troxell finished tilling between young vines, he was joined by his sons Noah and Calvin in the vineyard at Galen Glen Vineyard and Winery.

than fifty years, and during that time, the family never lost a crop to winter damage or spring frost, even though the land is 1,000 feet above sea level. The Troxells are hopeful that French hybrid grapes and some cold weather vinifera will be able to grow and thrive in their location.

While Galen does most of the vineyard work, the winemaking is primarily Sarah's responsibility. In 1998 the winery produced 1,500 gallons, and as their grapes come into production, the number of gallons will also increase. Each winter the Troxells try to tackle one large project. One year they lowered the floor of the potato cellar by digging down 3 feet in order to increase the vertical space for the wine tanks. During the winter of 1998–99, they finished the part of their basement that was to serve as the tasting room for the winery. Another project they may tackle in the future is converting an arched stone cellar near the winery building into a barrel storage facility.

Wine List

Dry: Chambourcin

Semidry: Vidal Blanc, Vin Gris of Chambourcin

Semisweet: Noah's Blush (Steuben), Winter Mountain White (Cayuga)

Best-selling Wine: Noah's Blush (named after Sarah and Galen's son)

Hours

Saturday, noon to 5:00 P.M. or by appointment.

Services and Events

Swing and climbing sets to entertain children while adults taste the wine.

Directions

From the intersection of Route 22 and Route 100, west of Allentown, go north on Route 100 until it intersects with Route 309. Turn left on Route 309, and go over the mountain ridge. At the intersection with Route 895, turn right and go east for about 3 miles. Turn left onto Troxell Valley Road. Continue about 2.3 miles, and turn right on Wintermountain Drive. The winery is on the right in 0.7 mile.

Glades Pike Winery

2706 Glades Pike, Somerset, PA 15501
PHONE: (814) 445-3753
FAX: (814) 445-1856
E-MAIL: addly@shol.com
WEBSITE: www.somersetcounty.com/winery/index.html

LOCATION: **Mountains, Southwest Area**

BEWARE OF WHAT WINEMAKING CLUB YOU JOIN—YOU MIGHT END UP THE owner of a winery! That's what happened to Steve and Karen Addleman. They and a group of friends started tasting wines on a regular basis and on fall weekends would tour wineries, sometimes as many as six or seven in two days. The winery bug bit hard, and nine of them decided to start a winery. They picked a location that was on a well-traveled highway near several resorts in the Laurel Highlands, east of Pittsburgh, and where one of the group owned a bed-and-breakfast inn with an old dairy barn dating back to 1868.

It took almost a year for the group to clean up the barn and renovate it so that it could be used for making wine. This involved cleaning out the accumulated manure, installing floor drains, and pouring a new concrete floor, plus cleaning the entire facility so that it would be ready for winemaking. Steve Addleman had a background in the dairy industry and had spent time supervising a laboratory doing quality control and quality assurance work. Since he had more of a scientific background, he became the head winemaker for the group.

The winery officially opened in April 1995. It wasn't long before it became apparent that there is truth in the saying "too many cooks spoil the broth." From the inception of the winery, the group had changing goals and other differences. Steve and Karen made arrangements to buy out six of their partners and in January 1998 became 80 percent owners of the winery. Fortunately for all concerned, the former owners remain good friends with the Addlemans, and when Steve needs a bottling crew or help with other projects, they will come to the winery and pitch in. He has additional assistance in Mike McVicker, who became the full-time winemaker in 1998. Both Steve and Karen have full-time jobs outside the winery, so Mike's presence has been very helpful, especially as the winery now has a production of 9,000 gallons.

The winery buys all of the grapes that it uses, and Steve plans to keep it that way. He recognizes that he doesn't have a green thumb, and furthermore, he really isn't interested in growing the grapes as much as he is in making the best-quality wines that he can.

The problem with using a barn as a winemaking facility is that it has a limited amount of space that can be used for the process. Though a barn may look big, a winery can fill it up rapidly. At the moment, this is the problem facing Steve at Glades Pike. The tank storage area is full, and the winery is producing its maximum number of gallons. Steve likes the winery's location and doesn't want to relocate, but he would like to increase production to 12,000 gallons. It is a dilemma that so far has not been resolved.

The tasting room is located in a sun-filled corner of the barn, with space for both wine and gift displays. It's a cheerful and pleasant place to taste through the wines.

Mike McVicker, winemaker, and Steve Addleman, owner of Glades Pike Winery, with their newly acquired bottling line.

Wine List

Dry: Léon Millot, Foch, DeChaunac, Seyval Blanc, Chardonnay

Semidry: Steuben, Vidal Blanc, Baco Noir

Semisweet: Bicentennial Blush (Niagara, Seyval, Vidal, and Concord), Glades Pike Red (Baco and Concord), Concord, Cayuga

Sweet: Diamond, Niagara

Fruit Wines: Spiced Apple, Cherry, Raspberry, Apple, Sparkling Apple Cider

Best-selling Wine: Bicentennial Blush

Hours

Daily, noon to 6:00 P.M.

Services and Events

Personalized labels, baskets, picnic tables, Open House weekends in the spring and fall featuring music, food, entertainment, and wine.

Directions

Glades Pike Winery is located east of Pittsburgh and south of the Pennsylvania Turnpike in the Laurel Highlands resort area. From Pittsburgh, go east on the Turnpike to exit 9, Donegal, and go east on Route 31 for 13 miles. The winery will be on the left. From Philadelphia, go west on the Turnpike to exit 10, Somerset, and continue west on Route 31 for 6 miles. The winery will be on the right.

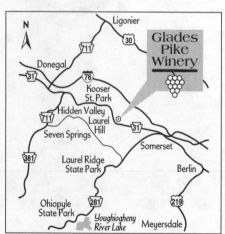

Extension

Exxon Plaza, Pennsylvania Turnpike exit 9, Donegal, (724) 593-1981 (open Sunday–Thursday, noon to 6:00 P.M.; Friday and Saturday, noon to 8:00 P.M.).

 Heritage Wine Cellars

12162 E. Main Rd., North East, PA 16428
PHONE: (814) 725-8015; outside PA: (800) 747-0083
FAX: (814) 725-8654
WEBSITE: www.heritagewine.com

LOCATION: Lake Erie

HERITAGE WINE CELLARS OPENED IN 1977 IN A RESTORED EIGHTEENTH-century barn not far from the intersection of I-90 and Route 20. The winery was originally started by three brothers—Robert, Michael, and William Bostwick—and is now owned by Bob and Bev Bostwick, who have recently been joined in the business by two sons, Joshua and Matthew. Matthew is the assistant winemaker. While some grapes are grown on the family farm, over 200 tons are purchased so that the winery can produce approximately 40,000 gallons per year. The Bostwicks cur-

Heritage Wine Cellars is housed in an eighteenth-century barn outside North East, Pennsylvania.

rently sell wine at three extensions: two in Pittsburgh, and one in a mall in Erie.

In the future, Bob would like to take advantage of his location near exit 12 of I-90 and develop a Williamsburg-style village, complete with craftspeople, to attract more visitors off the highway. In addition, he is considering holding a festival, possibly a jazz festival, sometime in the near future. The Bostwicks recently opened a seasonal restaurant at the winery named "The Gathering."

The original family farm dates back to 1833. Bob's father, Kenneth, converted the farm to grape growing, and today Bob manages 115 acres of grapes. The grapes grown are primarily Concord, but six other varieties are also under cultivation. Bob is slowly removing the Concord vines and replacing them with wine grapes, including DeChaunac, Chambourcin, and Cabernet Franc. Some of the soils on the farm are clay, and as a result, the vinifera and French hybrid grapes do not grow particularly well there.

Wine List

Dry: Chablis, Seyval Blanc, Vidal Blanc, White Riesling, Solebury White, Chardonnay, Cabernet Franc, Cabernet Sauvignon, Chancellor, Léon Millot, Burgundy (hybrid blend), Solebury Red

Semidry: Country Pink, Gladwin

Semisweet: Fredonia, Niagara, Delaware

Sweet: Sweet Country White, Pink Catawba, Sweet Rose, Isabella, Blush, Concord, Ice Wine of Vidal Blanc, Almondiera

Sparkling: Bubbling Catawba, Bubbling Niagara, Cold Goose (Concord), Peach Fuzz, Plum Crazy, Private Reserve, Very Beary Blackberry

Fruit Wines: Blueberry, Dark Cherry, Dutch Apple Wine, Dutch Apple Spiced Wine, Elderberry, Holiday Spice Wine, Kir (Current and Raspberry), Peach Wine, Raspberry, Sangria (citrus blend), Strawberry

Best-selling Wines: Concord, Niagara, Fredonia

Hours

May–December, Monday–Saturday, 9:00 A.M. to 6:00 P.M.; Sunday, 11:00 A.M. to 6:00 P.M.; January–April, Monday–Saturday, 10:00 A.M. to 5:00 P.M.; Sunday, noon to 5:00 P.M.

Directions

Take exit 12 from I-90; head north. Turn left on Route 20; the winery is on the right across from the McDonald's.

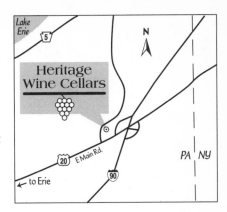

Services and Events

The Gathering, a restaurant located at the main winery in North East (open April 1 through December 31).

Extensions

- Heritage at Millcreek Mall the Bazaar Court, Millcreek Mall, (814) 864-9535.
- Heritage at Bell Vernon, 127 Speers Ave., Bell Vernon, (724) 483-3831.
- Heritage at McKeesport, 3806 O'Neal Rd., McKeesport (412) 672-0025.

Hunters Valley Winery

Box 326, R.D. #2, Liverpool, PA 17045
PHONE: (717) 444-7211
E-MAIL: dk.huntersvalley@worldnet.att.net

LOCATION: **Mountains, Central Area**

THERE IS AN OLD ADAGE IN THE WINE INDUSTRY THAT YOU SHOULD GROW grapes where grapes grow best and put the winery where the people are. Bill and Darlene Kvaternik ended up doing just that with their Hunters Valley Winery. The winery is located right on Route 15, the major north-south highway in central Pennsylvania, and big signs announce the existence of the winery to passing traffic. Most visitors never see the vineyards, which are located not quite half a mile up the hill behind the winery.

The Kvaterniks thought they wanted just to grow grapes and to make a little wine for their own consumption. In the early 1980s they purchased a small farm high on a hill, and they planted their first vines in 1981. The site had good air drainage, shale soils that drain well, and as a bonus, a wonderful view up and down the Susquehanna River valley and across to the Millersburg Ferry.

Originally the vineyard was planted with hybrids and native American grapes. The Seyval and Vidal grapes have done well, as have Dutchess, Catawba, and Delaware, and Chardonnay was added more recently. Two and a half acres are currently producing, and in the spring of 1999 the Kvaterniks planted another half acre, this time with Cabernet Franc. Bill would like to add more vinifera grapes, especially since it has become more difficult and expensive to purchase premium varieties such as Cabernet Sauvignon, Merlot, and Chambourcin.

Bill and Darlene originally planned to grow the grapes and sell them to home winemakers. What they didn't realize was that their grapes would ripen in August, when home winemakers are on vacation and not really interested in making wine. Since the Kvaterniks didn't have contracts with wineries to buy their grapes and had no facilities for cold storage to hold the grapes for amateur winemakers, one solution to the problem was to open a winery. They considered building a winery at the vineyard site but instead bought property below the vineyard directly on Route 15.

In 1986 the Kvaterniks opened Hunters Valley Winery, which is named for the local area. The winery itself is housed in a building that used to be a chick hatchery. The property also has a farmhouse, a building currently being used by a blacksmith, and a stone ruin that originally was a smokehouse for fish. The tasting room occupies the upper floor of the former hatchery, and the wine production area is in the basement. Though it is not a large space, the winery has room for tanks, barrels, and kegs of different sizes, along with other essential pieces of equipment for making wine. Outside, Bill has added a chilling room with a compressor to bring the temperature down so that finished wines can be stabilized.

Bill and Darlene recognize that they are tight on space, but they haven't decided what they want to do about it. In July 1999 Bill retired from his position as an environmental specialist for a housing agency in Harrisburg and now works full-time at the winery. Darlene plans to continue with her job as a social worker. The tasting room is run by Shirley Hartz, the winery's sales manager.

While production has grown to 3,000 gallons each harvest, the major problem for Hunters Valley is that the winery has difficulty keeping enough wine on hand to meet the demand. Their clientele is primarily

At one end of the tasting room, Darlene Kvaternik, co-owner of Hunters Valley Winery, labels wine bottles while Shirley Hartz, the winery's sales manager, creates wine gift baskets.

local—and very loyal—but people who are driving past on the highway also stop in.

Wine List

Dry: Chardonnay, Cabernet Franc, Berry Mountain Red (Chancellor, Baco Noir, and DeChaunac)

Semidry: Riesling, Seyval, Vidal, Heart of the Valley (Chancellor, Baco Noir, DeChaunac, and Vidal)

Semisweet: Susquehanna Sunrise, Concord

Sweet: Niagara, Country Spice

Best-selling Wine: Niagara

Hours

Wednesday, Thursday, and Saturday, 11:00 A.M. to 5:00 P.M.; Friday, 11:00 A.M. to 7:00 P.M.; Sunday, 1:00 to 5:00 P.M.

Services and Events

Specialty labels for weddings, other events, and holidays.

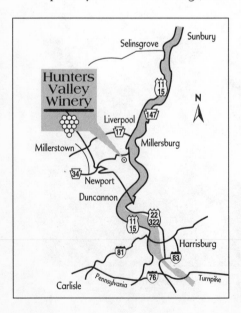

Directions

The winery is 26 miles north of Harrisburg on Routes 11/15. It is 2 miles south of the little town of Liverpool and 10 miles north of the intersection of Routes 22/322 and Routes 11/15.

Note: The state is in the process of rebuilding Routes 22/322 and Routes 11/15, and the section of Route 15 in front of the winery is being widened to four lanes. A jughandle intersection will allow access to the winery from both the north and the south when the project is finished.

🍇 In & Out Farm Vineyards

258 Durham Rd., Newtown, PA 18940
PHONE: (215) 860-5899
FAX: (215) 968-0941
E-MAIL: inout@voicenet.com

LOCATION: **Southeast, Philadelphia Area**

IN THE EARLY 1980S, THE SITE OF TODAY'S IN & OUT FARM VINEYARDS WAS a vegetable farm that had financial problems. Mike Selesnick ran a chemical company in New Jersey and wanted to diversify by acquiring property in Pennsylvania where he could have a stud farm—and a winery. He bought the farm in a bank sale, renovated the 1835 stone barn to include horse stalls, planted an acre of vines, and in 1984 started a small winery in the coach house. Mike now spends much of the year in Florida, but he returns to the winery for about five months and continues to be the winemaker.

Mike's son Bill currently lives on the farm and runs the winery. He is an artist, and some of his paintings are on exhibit in the winery. If he is available, he is quite willing to show interested customers a selection of his paintings in his house across the drive. The day-to-day operation of the winery is handled by Jim McLaughlin, who runs the tasting room and oversees the production of eight hundred to nine hundred cases of wine per year.

Visitors to the winery can see the small winery facility next door to the tasting room and then pay a call on Dancer's Victory, a racehorse worth about $1.5 million that has lived in the stud barn for the past three years, as well as several mares in a meadow adjacent to the vineyard. The acre vineyard is primarily for demonstration purposes; the winery purchases most of its grapes or juice.

Bill Selesnick and his son Elijah with some of Bill's paintings that hang on the walls of the tasting room at In & Out Vineyards.

Wine List

Dry: Chardonnay, Seyval, Chancellor Royale

Medium Dry: Vidal Blanc, Sparkling Vidal, Rose Bank Blush (Vidal)

Sweet: Niagara, Concord, Spice Wine (Chancellor with ginger, cinnamon, and cloves)

Best-selling Wine: Vidal Blanc

Hours

Saturday and Sunday, 11:00 A.M. to 5:00 P.M. (Weekdays by appointment.)

Services and Events

Special labels, art gallery, horses and stud farm.

Directions

In & Out Farm Vineyards is located in Bucks County north of Newtown. The winery is on the east side of Route 413, 1/2 mile north of the Newtown bypass and 3 miles south of Route 232. If you are driving north on Route 413, the driveway for the winery is on the right *before* the sign for the winery.

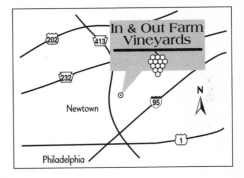

 Lancaster County Winery

Rawlinsville Rd., Willow Street, PA 17584
PHONE: (717) 464-3555

LOCATION: **Southeast, Susquehanna Valley**

LANCASTER COUNTY IS BLESSED WITH ROLLING HILLS AND BEAUTIFUL, lush green valleys. One of the lovely, tranquil spots along the banks of the Pequea Creek, south of the city of Lancaster, is the site of Lancaster County Winery. The farm dates back to 1718. The winery is in a barn that was built in 1815 and rebuilt in 1902, and the stone farmhouse was constructed in 1820.

In addition to being a historic site, Lancaster County Winery is one of the older wineries in the southeastern part of Pennsylvania. The original winery was owned by the Monsey Corporation, which was headed by H. Peterman Wood. Pete and Alice Wood operated the winery under the name Pequea Valley Vineyard and Winery for six years and, according to newspaper accounts, planted 30 acres of vineyard with a variety of hybrid grapes. During the 1970s the winery was plagued with financial problems, and it was finally sold in September 1988 at a sheriff's sale to the Commonwealth Bank and Trust Company of Williamsport.

In 1989 the winery was purchased by Dickel, Inc., a heating oil company in Valley Stream, New York. Todd Dickel at that time was president of Dickel, Inc., and he and his wife, Suzanne, moved to Willow Street to take over the property. The winery's name was changed to Lancaster County Winery, and for twenty years the Dickels have run it as a family business with their two children, Edward and Lynne. Under the ownership of the Dickels, the winery has continued to produce wines made from different hybrid varietals grown in their vineyard, which now totals 7 acres.

The tasting room and winery are located in the barn. The production facility is primarily in the basement, and the tasting room is on an upper level accessible directly from the driveway and parking lot. The walls of the main tasting room are decorated with antique wrought iron hinges and farm tools, and opposite the main door is a counter long enough to accommodate a busload of tourists. A large room to the left is used for wine and cheese tastings and other private parties. To the right is the wine shop, with bins containing the wines for sale and some other wine-related items. A list of wines, none of them vintage-dated, hangs on the wall above a small tasting bar in the wine shop, but when we visited the winery, there were no wines available for tasting. Since we did not taste through the wines, the wine list included here is a copy of the list above the tasting bar. According to Todd Dickel, all wines with "Colonial" in their name are sweet wines.

A Dalmatian barks his greeting to visitors at Lancaster County Winery.

Wine List

White: Rayon d'Or, Dry White Special Reserve, Vidal Blanc, White Chablis, Seyval Blanc

Blush/Rosé: Amber Blush, Pink Chablis

Red: Chelois, Foch, Dry Red Special Reserve, Cascade, Chancellor

Sweet: Colonial White, Colonial Sweet Pink, Colonial Spiced Apple, Colonial Red

Best-selling Wines: Sweet wines

Hours

Monday–Saturday, 10:00 A.M. to 4:00 P.M.; Sunday, 1:00 P.M. to 4:00 P.M.

Services and Events

Large room for functions, picnic tables.

Directions

From Lancaster, take Route 222 south, then continue south on Route 272 through Willow Street. Turn right on Baumgardner Road, and go 1 mile to Rawlinsville Road. Turn left, and the winery will be on the left in 2 miles.

Lapic Winery

902 Tulip Dr., New Brighton, PA 15066
PHONE: (724) 846-2031

LOCATION: **Mountains of Pennsylvania, southwest area**

PAUL AND JOSEPHINE LAPIC DESCRIBE THEIR WINERY AS A "HOBBY GONE wild." They began in 1977 by planting grapevines a few at a time, until they had 2 acres planted, and Paul's brother Walter also put in 2 acres of grapes on an adjoining property. At that time, Paul and Josie did all the work in the vineyard and the winery, with some assistance from their four sons. Today Paul and Josie are not as involved as they once were. Two of their sons, Mike and Paul J., have taken over the vineyard and winery management, and the winemaking is handled by Craig Rowland. They now run the tasting room and gradually will also take over the marketing end of the business.

The Lapics expanded the winery from an initial production of 1,800 gallons to over 14,000 gallons, when they were supplying both the winery tasting room and an extension at a nearby mall. The second location proved to be too expensive to run in both time and money, and sales are now only at the winery, which currently produces about 10,000 gallons. The vineyard has remained the same size, and as a result, the Lapics have to purchase additional grapes and juice from Erie County growers. While their wine list includes some dry wines, most are semidry or semisweet, because that's what their customers tend to prefer.

When you watch people in the tasting room, it soon becomes apparent that Paul and Josie know almost everyone who comes in and often can anticipate what each customer will want. Sales most often are by the half case or the case. Another aspect of the Lapics' personalized service for their customers is the many special label wines they provide for local businesses or for events such as weddings.

Paul and Josephine Lapic in the tasting room at Lapic Winery.

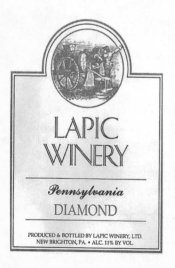

Wine List

Dry: Vidal Blanc, Seyval Blanc, Cayuga, Riesling, Baco Noir, Chambourcin

Semidry: Classic Red, Steuben

Medium dry: Blush de Blanc, Red Harvest, White Harvest

Semisweet: Pink Catawba, Concord, Diamond, Valley Red, Valley White, Valley Rosé, Sweet Heart

Best-selling Wines: Semisweet wines

Hours

January–February, 10:00 A.M. to 5:00 P.M.; March–December, Monday–Friday, 10:00 A.M. to 6:00 P.M.; Saturday, 10:00 A.M. to 5:00 P.M.; Sunday, 1:00 P.M. to 5:00 P.M.

Services and Events

Specialized labels, festival in early October.

Directions

Take I-79 north from Pittsburgh to the exit for Route 68 and Zelienople. Go west on Route 68 for approximately 9 miles. Watch for winery signs, and turn right on Tulip Drive. The winery is just over the top of the hill on the left.

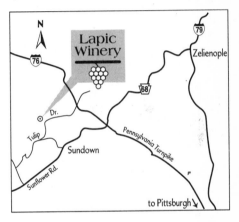

Laurel Mountain Vineyard

R.D. 1, Box 238, Falls Creek, PA 15840
PHONE AND FAX: (814) 371-7022
E-MAIL: laurlmtn@penn.com
WEBSITE: www.wmcdata.com/laurel

LOCATION: **Mountains, Northwest Area**

WHEN JOHN AND BARBARA NORDBERG DECIDED THEY WANTED TO GROW some grapes and maybe someday open a winery, they had one advantage: John's family had owned a farm in northwestern Pennsylvania near the town of Driftwood since 1907. The farm had a southern exposure and consisted of 400 acres, some of which could be planted with grapes. It also seemed to have a favorable microclimate, as the temperatures there were often warmer than in other nearby areas, even those farther to the south.

But there was one problem: The farm is accessible only by fording the Sinnamahoning River—there is no bridge for cars and trucks. From the end of November until the river level drops, usually in May, there is no way to get to or from the farm, except to walk across a railroad bridge. While grapes might grow there, it definitely was not a good site for a winery because of its inaccessibility and the lack of a population base nearby. The Nordbergs solved the problem by purchasing another small farm just north of I-80 and the exit for DuBois, which has a population, including the surrounding area, of approximately 35,000 people. In 1994 they moved from Washington, D.C., to the DuBois area. They opened the winery in November 1995, and are especially proud of their knowledgeable and friendly staff.

John and Barbara began planting grapes on the farm by the river in 1986 and now are growing approximately 20 acres of vineyard with thirty-five different varieties. They are the only grape growers in Cameron County, and when they put in the first Foch and Seyval vines, they had no idea what would be able to survive the climate. After thirteen years of experience, it appears that some French hybrids can do well there, as well as some of the native American varieties. Riesling is the only vinifera grape that may survive in that location. While many Pennsylvania vineyands have birds or deer that like to eat young vines or ripe grapes, the Nordbergs have an additional problem in their vineyard—elk—and have had to install a fence to keep the animals out. The elk fence is similar to an electric deer fence, except that the wires are heavier.

Because of the inaccessibility of the Driftwood vineyard location, the winery opened in the old barn of the Nordberg's farm near DuBois. It soon became apparent that the winery production facility and the tasting room needed more space, and so a new building was constructed in 1998. The wine tanks are now mostly located in this addition, as is John's antique tool museum, which showcases his collection of old tools, many of which had been used on the family farm. Visitors to the winery are welcome to tour the museum and try to figure out what five mystery tools are and how they were used. Anyone who identifies all five correctly will be rewarded with a free bottle of Concord or Niagara wine, but so far the Nordbergs have had to give only four bottles away.

Wine List

Dry: Vidal, Chardonnay, Foch, Cabernet Sauvignon

Semisweet: Seyval, Riesling, Vignoles, Delaware, Mountain Mist (Delaware, Niagara, and Catawba), Niagara, Bucktrail White (50

Barbara Nordberg manages the tasting room on the first floor of the winery building at Laurel Mountain Vineyard. An extensive wine gift shop is located on the second floor.

percent Seyval plus a vineyard blend of white varietals), Treasure Lake White (Delaware, Niagara, Seyval, and Apple), Bucktrail Red (Concord, Fredonia, and Foch), Rattlesnake Red (Fredonia, Foch, Niagara, and Steuben), Treasure Lake Red (vineyard blend of ten hybrid varietals), Laurel Blush (Catawba and Fredonia), Rosé (Steuben)

Sweet: Concord, Punxy Tawnic (Fredonia plus spices), Ruby Red (blend of native American grapes)

Fruit Wines: Apple, Groundhog Grog (spiced Apple), Peach, Cherry

Best-selling Wines: Mountain Mist, Groundhog Grog, Bucktrail Red

Hours

Wednesday–Sunday, 10:00 A.M. to 6:00 P.M.

Services and Events

Personalized labels, gift baskets, gift and craft shop, antique tool museum.

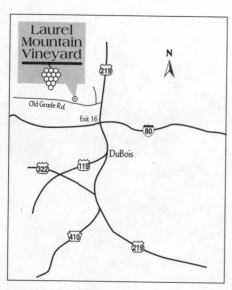

Directions

The winery is just off I-80 north of DuBois. Take I-80 to exit 16. Go north on Route 219 toward Brockway for 1 1/2 miles. Turn left at the first intersection onto Old Grade Road. The winery is on the right in 2 miles.

Manatawny Creek Winery

227 Levengood Rd., Douglassville, PA 19518
PHONE: (610) 689-9804
FAX: (610) 689-9838
E-MAIL: manatawny@aol.com
WEBSITE: www.manatawnycreekwinery.com

LOCATION: Southeast, Lehigh Valley

THE MAJOR ROAD BETWEEN READING AND PHILADELPHIA IS ROUTE 422, and only a few miles off the highway is a brand new winery named after the creek that runs nearby. An Indian word, *Manatawny* is translated approximately as "where we meet to drink." The Levengood family, which owns Manatawny Creek Winery, hopes that many people both locally and from the highway will come to taste, buy, and drink their wines. The farm that is home to the new winery has been in the Levengood family since the early 1900s, and three generations of Levengoods are now involved in the winery's operation.

The winery is actually an eight-person corporation. Ralph and Pearl Levengood own the farm where the winery is located. Their son Darvin and his wife, Mary, are involved in the day-to-day operation of the winery, with Mary running the tasting room and Darvin helping with all aspects of the vineyard and the winery. Darvin's sister, Roberta Rohn, and her husband, Richard, live in West Virginia and help at the winery on a more limited basis for special events or the harvest. Joanne Levengood, Darvin and Mary's daughter, and her husband, Ted Naccarella, are the third generation participating in this new venture. Ted is a patent attorney, and when Joanne decided she no longer wanted to pursue her field, environmental engineering, the two moved to California so that Joanne could attend the University of California at Davis and work toward a master's degree in enology. During several harvest seasons, she worked with Kent Rasmussen at Kent Rasmussen Winery and also at Stags Leap Wine Cellars in California. Joanne and Ted began to think about moving back to Pennsylvania to be closer to family, and in July 1998 Joanne's dream of having a family winery on her grandparents' farm became a reality.

The winery at Manatawny Creek Winery is a family project (from left): mother, Mary Levengood; son-in-law, Ted Naccarella; daughter, Joanne; and father, Darvin. Not pictured are the owners of the property, grandparents Ralph and Pearl Levengood.

Rather than convert an existing structure into a winery facility, the Levengoods selected a hillside site overlooking the Manatawny Creek for a new building whose organization and purpose would be for winemaking and wine sales. The resulting winery is built into the hill, with the winery portion partly underground. Access to the tasting room, on the top floor, is directly off the parking lot outside.

The Levengoods would like to grow to about five thousand cases (11,000 gallons). They want to produce what they can sell at the winery and through nearby restaurants, while living up to the meaning of their name, "where we meet to drink"—and to taste well-crafted wine.

The Levengoods already have 6 acres with producing wine grapes, including Cayuga, Vidal, Seyval, Chancellor, Foch, and Steuben. In 1998 and 1999, 4 more acres were planted in a new vineyard on the hill above the winery. The total acreage of the farm is 88 acres, and vineyard plantings may someday take 15 acres of that space. The farm also grows blueberries, blackberries, raspberries, and apples, all of which are used to some extent for wine.

The tasting room is a spacious facility with windows looking down toward the Manatawny Creek and interior windows that give visitors an opportunity to observe winery activities happening in the winery facility below.

Vidal Blanc, an off-dry, German-style white wine bottled in a cobalt blue bottle, is the winery's best-selling wine. The Levengoods have found that both the wine and its blue bottle are quite popular with customers.

Wine List

Dry: Chardonnay, Cabernet Franc

Semidry: Cayuga White, Vidal Blanc, Autumn Blush (Steuben), Harvest Red (Foch, Chancellor, and other red hybrids)

Sweet: Niagara, Concord

Fruit Wines: Cherry, Peach, Blueberry, Blackberry, Spiced Apple

Best-selling Wine: Vidal Blanc

Hours

Friday and Saturday, 10:00 A.M. to 6:00 P.M.; Sunday, noon to 6:00 P.M.

Directions

From Route 422 between King of Prussia and Reading, exit at Route 662 North in Douglassville. Go north on Route 662 for 3 miles. Turn right on Blacksmith Road, and make the first right onto Levengood Road. The winery is on the right in 0.8 mile.

Mazza Vineyards

11815 E. Lake Rd., North East, PA 16428
PHONE: (814) 725-8695 or (800) 796-WINE
FAX: (814) 725-3948
WEBSITE: www.mazzawines.com

LOCATION: Lake Erie
(Lake Erie Quality Wine Alliance)

TWENTY-FIVE YEARS AGO ERIE COUNTY WAS GROWING THOUSANDS OF acres of grapes, primarily Concords for use by Welch's, but had only two wineries, Presque Isle Wine Cellars and Penn Shore Vineyards. At that time the Mazza brothers, Bob and Frank, were involved in the family construction business and also managed their father's 20-acre grape farm. Their interest stimulated by the two new Erie County wineries, and encouraged by Walter Taylor of Bully Hill Winery in New York, Bob and Frank decided to open their own winery. They built the Mediterranean-style winery with the help of cellarmaster Gary Mosier in 1973 and formally opened in 1974.

One of their early decisions was to hire Helmut Kranich, a graduate of Geisenheim Institute in Germany, as their winemaker. Almost immediately Kranich made a name for Mazza wines. Backed by the Mazzas' philosophy of producing the best possible wines, and with his experience in Germany, he made a Riesling in 1974 that received national recognition. The 1974 Riesling was entered in a wine tasting in Chicago where the object was to identify a bottle of German Riesling from the Mosel region from the many other entries. The Mazza Riesling was voted most likely to be the German Mosel; this achievement received widespread attention when *Chicago Tribune* columnist Ruth Ellen Church reported the story.

In the years since that Riesling put Mazza Vineyards on the wine map, many changes have taken place. Kranich stayed as winemaker for five years, and then Gary Mosier took over his responsibilities. In 1980 Bob became the owner of Mazza Vineyards and Frank acquired an interest in Mount Hope Winery in southeastern Pennsylvania. Later, in 1983, Bob took over the management of Penn Shore Vineyards. More recently, Bob has started a fresh juice business that now supplies about

45,000 gallons to wineries from Connecticut to Virginia and as far away as Nebraska and Iowa.

Mazza Vineyards now produces between 25,000 and 30,000 gallons of wine per year and sells it at the winery, through the Pennsylvania State Stores, and at two extensions. "We don't try to sell all our wines at the State Stores," Bob notes. "I try to put in wines that fill a niche in the State Store product mix. As a result, our number one seller there is our Niagara." When the law was changed in Pennsylvania to allow several wineries to get together to market their wines in one location, Bob joined forces with Penn Shore and Presque Isle Wine Cellars to open a joint wine shop in Erie. "We've found that sales have really increased at the winery, and we don't need to open more extensions, but having this location in Erie has been a good move for us," says Bob.

Bob has also been active with the Lake Erie Quality Wine Alliance, a group of wineries in Ohio, Pennsylvania, and New York that have come together to promote the Lake Erie region as a major wine-producing area. Recently, Bob and his wife, Kathie, and another couple opened the Grape Arbor Inn, a bed and breakfast in North East that provides a con-

Bob Mazza and winemaker Gary Mosier contemplate the flavors in one of the red wines at Mazza Vineyards.

venient and comfortable base from which to visit all the wineries in the North East area. Bob plans to expand the visitor education area and the production part of the winery.

Mazza Vineyards has approximately 9 acres planted, most of it in Vidal and DeChaunac, plus some Pinot Gris, Cabernet Franc, St. Vincent, and Chambourcin. When we visited the winery in November 1998, Bob had left 3 tons of Vidal grapes hanging on the vines to make ice wine. Ice wine is a dessert-style sweet wine that has become quite popular, especially at wineries in Ontario and around Lake Erie, and Mazza Vineyards has developed a following for theirs. Ice wine is made from grapes that are left hanging on the vines after the end of the growing season. Gradually, as the weather cools, the grape berries shrivel and desiccate, which concentrates the sugars in the juice. When the temperature falls to about 22 to 23 degrees Fahrenheit, the water that remains in the juice freezes, and the grapes are ready to be picked and immediately pressed. Because the grapes have been drying out on the vine, the quantity of juice they produce is much less than from grapes picked during the regular harvest, and the juice that results is more concentrated in flavors and much higher in sugar content. Grapes for ice wine usually are picked in December or early January, depending on when the temperature falls low enough to freeze the grapes. Ice wine was originally made in Germany whenever the weather cooperated in freezing the grapes left hanging on the vine to the proper temperature. The weather around the Great Lakes is more consistent and allows traditional ice wines to be made on a more regular basis. Since 1984, when he made his first ice wine, Bob has made the wine every year except 1995 and 1997.

MAZZA VINEYARDS
ICE WINE OF VIDAL BLANC
PENNSYLVANIA

Alcohol 10% by Volume   Residual 13% by Weight
Produced and Bottled by
MAZZA VINEYARDS, NORTH EAST, PENNSYLVANIA

Wine List

Dry: Seyval Blanc, Chardonnay, Vineyard Country Chablis, Chambourcin, Cabernet Sauvignon, Cabernet Franc, Commemorative Red

Semidry: Riesling Champagne, Riesling, Cayuga, Vineyard Country Blush

Semisweet: Champagne, Vidal Blanc, Vineyard Country Gold, Vineyard Country Red, Vineyard Country Rose, Concord

Sweet: Late Harvest Vidal, Ice Wine of Vidal Blanc, Pink Catawba, Niagara

Fruit and Specialty Wines: Holiday, Spiced Apple, Draft Apple Cider, Strawberry, Peach, Cherry, Pear, Red Raspberry, Sonatina—Bubbling Rose, Sonatina—Bubbling White

Best-selling Wine: Niagara

Hours

July–August, Monday–Saturday, 9:00 A.M. to 8:00 P.M.; Sunday, 11:00 A.M. to 4:30 P.M.; September–June, Monday–Saturday, 9:00 A.M. to 5:30 P.M.; Sunday, 11:00 A.M. to 4:30 P.M.

Directions

Take exit 11 off I-90, and head north toward Lake Erie and North East. Cross Route 20 and continue to Route 5. Turn right, and go about 2 miles. The winery is on the right.

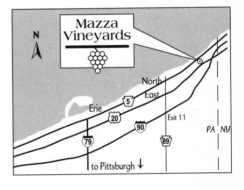

Extensions

- The Vintage Line Wine Shop, 2006 W. Eighth St., Erie, (814) 452-3697.
- Naturally Yours Gourmet Foods & Gifts, 3741 W. 26th St., Erie, a joint outlet with Penn Shore Vineyards and Presque Isle Wine Cellars, (814) 835-5255 (open Monday–Friday, 10:00 A.M. to 8:30 P.M.; Saturday, 10:00 A.M. to 4:00 P.M.; Sunday, noon to 4:00 P.M.).

Mount Hope Estate and Winery

83 Mansion House Rd., Manheim, PA 17545
PHONE: (717) 665-7021, ext. 129

LOCATION: Southeast, Susquehanna Valley

FROM ITS BEGINNING IN 1980, MOUNT HOPE ESTATE AND WINERY HAS been more than just a winery. The site of the winery was the historic Grubb Mansion, built in 1800 by Henry Bates Grubb, son of one of Colonial America's wealthiest ironmasters, as the summer home for his family. Three generations of Grubbs lived in the mansion, and after it was sold in 1885, the new owners expanded it to thirty-two rooms and added Victorian decor, including Egyptian marble fireplaces, ceiling murals, turrets, and a grand ballroom.

Visitors to the winery paid $2 to tour the mansion, ending up in the tasting room to sample the wine. While tours of the mansion were a successful draw, Chuck Romito and his partners in the wine business began to add other special events to attract people to the winery. Their location only half a mile from an exit of the Pennsylvania Turnpike provided tourists with easy access, and an arts and crafts festival held only three months after the winery opened was attended by more than ten thousand people.

Another special event in 1981 was a one-day jousting tournament. It proved to be so successful that the following year the winery held a Renaissance Faire, a re-creation of a sixteenth-century English country fair, over Memorial Day weekend. This event attracted six thousand people, and within a short time, the Renaissance Faire was expanded to cover multiple weekends—and the business of Mount Hope became more about entertainment than about wine. In 1998, more than 150,000 people came to the Renaissance Faire and another 75,000 attended the other special events at Mount Hope. Eight days were set aside as special school event days, and some 5,000 children participated in the Faire on each of these days. The Renaissance Faire has been listed as one of the top ten attractions in the state by the Pennsylvania Chamber of Commerce; in 1997 the Faire was recognized by the *American Amusement Magazine* as one of 250 top events in the country; and in 1998 it was named one of the top 100 events nationwide by the American Bus Association. Mount Hope hires a professional cast of about forty people and relies on a volunteer company of another sixty to seventy in order to stage these events.

Though wine is no longer the main focus at Mount Hope Estate and Winery, Chuck Romito continues to produce 30,000 gallons per year. The vines that were planted in 1980 between the mansion and the highway were pulled out in 1992 to make room for more parking lots for the Renaissance Faire, and the wine is now made in North East, Pennsylvania, by Mazza Vineyards. But according to Chuck, wine is still important to Mount Hope. It is sold retail only, not through the State Store system or in restaurants, and people often buy the wine as a memento of a special outing to one of the Mount Hope events.

Wine List

Dry: Mount Hope Red, Chardonnay, Classic Vidal Blanc

Semidry: Chablis, Rosé, Riesling, Vidal Blanc, Seyval Blanc

Visitors to the Mount Hope Estate and Winery may taste the wine in the wine shop (on the left), tour the Grubb Mansion, or attend one of the winery's festivals such as the popular Renaissance Faire.

Semisweet: Sauterne, Burgundy, Concord

Sweet: Pink Catawba, Niagara, Vignoles

Sparkling: Champagne *(méthode champenoise)*, Pizzaz Blanc, Pizzaz Rouge, Pizzaz Cassis

Specialty Wines: Holiday, Pennsylvania Dutch Spiced Apple, May Wine, Sangria, Nouveau, Strawberry Wine, Peach Wine, Cherry Wine

Best-selling Wines: Concord, Pink Catawba, Niagara

Hours

January–July, Monday–Saturday, 10:00 A.M. to 5:00 P.M.; Sunday, noon to 5:00 P.M.; August–December, Monday–Friday, 10:00 A.M. to 5:00 P.M.; Saturday–Sunday, 9:00 A.M. to 7:00 P.M.

Services and Events

Extensive entertainment facilities, with special theaters and buildings for different events, festivals, Renaissance Faire.

Directions

From the Pennsylvania Turnpike: Take exit 20 and go south on Route 72 for 1/2 mile. The winery is on the left.

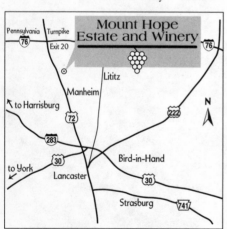

From Lancaster: Take Route 72 north for 14 miles. The winery is on the right.

Extension

Mount Hope Wine Gallery, Route 340, Intercourse, (717) 768-7194 (open Monday–Saturday, 10:00 A.M. to 6:00 P.M.; Sunday, 11:00 A.M. to 6:00 P.M.).

Mount Nittany Vineyard & Winery

R.D. 1, Box 138, 300 Houser Rd., Centre Hall, PA 16828
PHONE: (814) 466-6373
FAX: (814) 466-3066
E-MAIL: jlc10@psu.edu

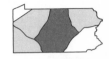

LOCATION: Mountains, Central Area

IN 1983 JOE AND BETTY CARROLL MOVED TO A 65-ACRE FARM NOT FAR from State College. They were looking for a change of lifestyle, away from the traffic that passed by their house even in the relatively small town that is home to the Pennsylvania State University. They considered raising trees, horses, or grapes. Grapes won out, and in 1984 the Carrolls planted 2½ acres of Vidal, Cayuga, Seyval, Chardonnay, and DeChaunac, with the intention of selling whatever grapes they produced to local wineries and amateur winemakers. For several years, that's what happened: Joe continued to teach at Penn State, and the Carrolls sold their grapes. It soon became apparent that they were producing more grapes than could readily be sold, so Joe and Betty changed their plans and opened Mount Nittany Vineyard & Winery in 1990.

Joe retired from teaching in 1992 and gradually increased the size of the winery to the point where today it is producing nearly 10,000 gallons. The vineyard has been expanded to 5 acres, but in order to meet the demand for their wines, the Carrolls also have to purchase some grapes, both from the Erie region and from southeastern Pennsylvania. They have hired two full-time people to help out in the vineyard and the winery: Carl Helrich, who describes himself as a "winemaker in training," and Sandy Alexander.

The Carrolls' wine marketing takes advantage of the winery's proximity to Penn State. The winery is named for Mount Nittany, a prominent local geologic landmark that slopes up from the vineyards to the north. The winery's most popular wine, Tailgate Red, reflects the Penn State affection for football and the popularity of partying in the parking lot before, during, and after a game. Three other wines, the Nittany Mountain White, Nittany Mountain Red, and Nittany Mountain Blush,

The Swiss-style winery building at Mount Nittany Vineyard & Winery has a view not only of the vineyards, but across the valley to a ski area outside State College.

all capitalize on Penn State loyalties and identification. The Carrolls are considering putting the Nittany Mountain White in a cobalt blue bottle to extend the identification with Penn State colors.

The winery facility has grown as needed to handle the increase in production. The tasting room is still in a large room that overlooks the vineyards and has a view of the local ski slope on Tussey Mountain to the south. The winery production area below the tasting room has had several additions and now resembles a Maine farmhouse, with the main house attached to the garage, which is adjacent to the workshop that leads to the barn, all strung out in one long, attached row. The most recent building project is at the far end. The Carrolls knew they needed more bottle and equipment storage, so when they added on that space, they also added a second floor with a large room for banquets.

Wine List

Dry: Chardonnay, Chardonnay Reserve, Pinot Gris, Proprietors Select White (mostly Seyval and Chardonnay), Seyval Blanc, Cabernet Sauvignon, Cabernet Franc, Proprietors Select Red (Cabernet Franc

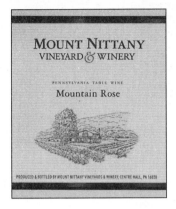

and Léon Millot), Nittany Mountain Red (DeChaunac and Cabernet Franc), and Chambourcin

Semidry: Nittany Mountain White (Cayuga, Seyval, and Vidal), Bergwein (Cayuga and Riesling), Tailgate Red (mostly DeChaunac with some Léon Millot)

Semisweet: Nittany Mountain Blush (Cayuga, Seyval, Vidal, and some red wine for color), Mountain Rose (Concord blend), Mountain Mist (Niagara blend)

Sweet: Niagara, Autumn Nectar (primarily Vignoles and Vidal), Spy Swine (blend of white wines plus spices)

Best-selling Wine: Tailgate Red

Hours

Tuesday–Friday, 1:30 to 5:00 P.M.; Saturday, 10:00 A.M. to 5:00 P.M.; Sunday, 12:30 to 4:00 P.M. (Closed on major holidays and during January.)

Services and Events

Picnic area, dining area for catered events (up to sixty-five people).

Directions

The winery is about 7 miles east of State College in central Pennsylvania. From Route 322, turn east on Route 45. After passing the Elks Country Club on the right, immediately turn left onto Linden Hall Road. Go around the bend, down the hill, take a right at the pond onto Rock Hill Road, and go through the village of Linden Hall. Turn left onto Brush Valley Road

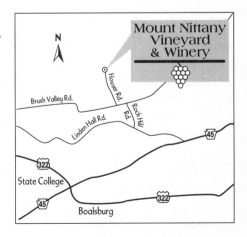

just before the church, then turn right on Houser Road toward the mountain. Go through the woods and up the lane to the winery.

Naylor Wine Cellars

4069 Vineyard Rd., Stewartstown, PA 17363-8478
PHONE: (800) 292-3370
FAX: (717) 993-9460
E-MAIL: sale@naylorwine.com
WEBSITE: www.naylorwine.ne.com

LOCATION: Southeast, Susquehanna Valley
(Mason-Dixon Wine Trail)

IF YOU MEET DICK NAYLOR AT NAYLOR WINE CELLARS, YOU MAY BE reminded of Santa Claus. Not only are the gray-white beard and the twinkle in the eye reminiscent of St. Nick, but Dick's pack is full—not of toys, but of a hundred different ways to sell wine. He opened his winery twenty years ago in 1979, and since then he has used a wide variety of creative ideas to promote and sell his product.

Dick's labels have been innovative from early in the winery's history. He called his Niagara wine the Golden Grenadier (after the Bureau of Alcohol, Tobacco and Firearms refused to approve the name Golden Hand Grenade) and put drawings of several biplanes and a World War I soldier holding aloft a bunch of grapes on the label. Early in the 1980s he created a new descriptor for his sweet wines: He called them "socially sweet," implying the context in which those wines might be enjoyed— casually, with friends, not with wine snobs. Some of his wines bear tongue-in-cheek names, such as Ekem, a sweet dessert wine made from Vignoles whose name is a play on the name of a winery in France, Chateau d'Yquem in Burgundy, that makes a Sauterne.

On another occasion, Dick invented a new product at a festival where he was not allowed to sell customers glasses of wine or bottles to be opened and consumed there. Using a snowball machine owned by a friend to make shaved ice, he created the Naylor Strawberry Wine Slushee. Less than an ounce of wine plus sugar water and some other ingredients for flavor and color were poured on the ice in a 6-ounce insulated coffee cup, and the slushee was ready to be consumed on a hot day!

Dick Naylor's involvement with wine goes back to his first days as a salesman, when he found out he could make a good impression by buying wine for his clients. He made his first wine in 1972—out of dandelions. In 1973 he planted twenty vines; two years later he bought a farm in York County and started planting vines by the acre. Naylor Wine Cellars opened in 1979 with 1,600 gallons of wine and a 10-acre vineyard. A new winery building was constructed in 1983 and a second building was finished in 1991. Today the vineyard has 33 acres planted, and the winery has grown to almost 20,000 gallons.

The winery initially was a partnership consisting of Dick and his wife, Audrey. Ted Potter, their son-in-law, soon joined the family business and today is involved in the daily management of the winery and as winemaker. A daughter, Janey, helps with office work and in the winery. Dick continues to handle marketing and do the wine blending.

Dick's marketing efforts have expanded as the winery grew in size. He has organized International Volksmarches—ten to twenty kilometer walks over a planned course—that are sponsored by the winery. Each year he has two festivals, one to celebrate the grape blossoms and one during harvest. After starting a series of big-band concerts, he discovered

Dick Naylor, on inspection, walks between the barrels and tanks at Naylor Wine Cellars in York County.

that people liked not only to listen to the music, but to dance as well. As a result, he built a pavilion to accommodate the musicians and a sizable dance floor for the customers. The first music evenings drew about one hundred people; in 1998 five evenings attracted more than five hundred. Dick plans to add more dance floor area and another deck to provide additional tables and chairs in something like a nightclub setting. Catered food and Naylor wine are available for each of these events.

NAYLOR

19   98

YORK COUNTY
Johannisberg Riesling
10.6% ALCOHOL BY VOLUME
PRODUCED AND BOTTLED BY NAYLOR WINE CELLARS, INC.
4069 VINEYARD ROAD, STEWARTSTOWN, PA 17363

Wine List

Dry: York White Rose (Vidal, Seyval, and Cayuga), Vidal Perfection, Pinot Gris, Chardonnay, Reserve Chardonnay, Nouveau (Chambourcin), Chambourcin, Cabernet Franc, Pinot Noir, Cabernet Sauvignon, Cabernet Sauvignon Reserve, Barone IV (Cabernet Sauvignon, Pinot Noir, Chambourcin, and Landal), Seductivo (75 percent Chambourcin and 25 percent Cabernet Sauvignon)

Semidry: Rhinelander (Vidal, Seyval, and Niagara), Blush (Vidal and DeChaunac), Rose O'Dechaunac (DeChaunac and Vidal), First Capital (four red varietals)

Sweet: Niagara, Muscat du Moulin (Muscat), Ekem (Vignoles), Johannisberg Riesling, Catawba, Holiday Spiced (Catawba with cinnamon and cloves), Concord, Intimacy (Vignoles Ice Wine), Essence of Chambourcin, Ambrosia's Dulce (Peach, Apple, and Concord)

Sparkling: Sparkling Niagara, Sparkling Viva (Vidal)

Best-selling Wines: York White Rose, Niagara, Concord

Hours

Monday–Saturday, 11:00 A.M. to 6:00 P.M.; Sunday, noon to 5:00 P.M.

Services and Events

Special food events, live big-band and rock music on summer evenings, a bi-monthly wine club, festivals in June and October, personalized labels, gift baskets.

Directions

Naylor Wine Cellars is located south of York, not far from the Pennsylvania-Maryland line. Take exit 1 off I-83. Go east on Route 851 to Stewartstown. Turn left onto Route 24. After 2 miles, turn left on Vineyard Road. The winery is on the right at the top of the hill in about 1/2 mile.

Extensions

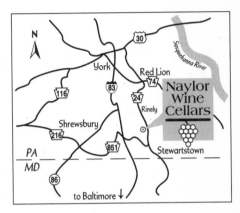

- Meadowbrook Village (in the pavilion next to Isaac's), Whiteford Rd., York (717) 755-9397 (open Monday–Saturday, 10:00 A.M. to 9:00 P.M.; Sunday, noon to 5:00 P.M.).
- Morningstar Marketplace, 5309 Lincoln Hwy. West (Route 30 east of York), Thomasville (open Saturday, 7:00 A.M. to 5:00 P.M.).

Nissley Vineyards

140 Vintage Dr., Bainbridge, PA 17502
PHONE: (717) 426-3514; in PA only, (800) 522-2387
FAX: (717) 426-1391

LOCATION: **Southeast, Susquehanna Valley**

WHEN YOU ARRIVE AT NISSLEY VINEYARDS, ONE OF THE FIRST QUESTIONS from the tasting room staff will be whether you'd like to take a tour of the vineyards and the winery. You'll then be handed a notebook with laminated pages of photographs and descriptions of what you'll see along the various stops on your tour. The tour takes you past an old limekiln that dates back to the nineteenth century, out to a nearby vineyard, and back through the converted and expanded tobacco barn that serves as the winery facility, ending in the tasting room.

Nissley Vineyards is one of the older wineries in Pennsylvania, with a history that goes back more than twenty years. The winery opened in 1978 after the grapes in the vineyard began to produce in enough quantity to make wine.

Dick Nissley had been in the bridge construction business in Pennsylvania for thirty-two years, and when he retired, he planned to play bridge, do some hunting and fishing, and grow some grapes on one of his farms. Meanwhile, Dick's son John, who had majored in agronomy at Penn State, returned from a three-year cross-country trip. John agreed to grow the grapes if Dick wanted to pursue his interest in making wines for sale. As a result, in 1975 John expanded Dick's original 2-acre vineyard by planting almost 27 acres of French hybrid grapes, including Aurore, Seyval, Vidal, DeChaunac, and Chancellor. When the winery opened in July 1978, Dick Nissley was definitely no longer retired, but a full-time winemaker and winery owner, and John became the vineyard manager. Other members of the family, including Dick's wife, Anna Ruth, and two of their daughters, Judy and Joyce, also became involved.

Today the winery is still run by the Nissley family, although Dick is no longer active in the winery management, and Anna Ruth, while retaining her role as secretary, does not spend as much time in the office and

Judy Nissley pours a sample of Nissley Vineyards' Cabernet Franc on a beautiful spring afternoon.

tasting room as she once did. The second generation is now responsible for the winery: Judy is the winery president, John is vice president and vineyard manager, Joyce is treasurer, and a third daughter, Mary Lee, is the winery shop manager.

Six years after planting the original vineyard, the Nissleys added 3 acres of vinifera grapes. They quickly discovered that Chardonnay, Riesling, and Gewürztraminer suffered severe winter damage on their site, and later plantings were all French hybrid grapes, such as Vidal, Cayuga, Vignoles, Chambourcin, and Baco Noir, plus native American varieties, including Niagara, Concord, and Catawba. More recently, they added a small amount of Cabernet Franc, and it has done so well that they plan to plant more. Currently the vineyard has 50 acres planted out of 150 acres that are suitable for grapes.

The winery facility is constructed in a style that Judy Nissley calls "Pennsylvania Dutch Mediterranean." A tobacco barn was substantially altered and a large addition was added, complete with a stone front on the building with six arches that make the building both distinctive and nonbarnlike in appearance. Dick originally used milk tanks and chocolate conching tanks for fermenting and storing the wines; those tanks are still in use today. The winemaker, Bill Gulvin, has recently added some square tanks that make better use of the limited space in the winery. Bill, who has been at Nissley Vineyards for seven years, came with fifteen years of experience making wine in New York State.

The winery now produces about 35,000 gallons of wine each year. The first wines the Nissleys made were almost exclusively dry, but they soon realized that some of their local customers preferred sweeter wines. Today their wine list offers customers a range from dry to sweet.

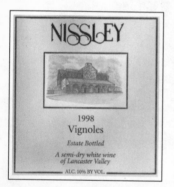

NISSLEY

1998
Vignoles

Estate Bottled

*A semi-dry white wine
of Lancaster Valley*

ALC. 10% BY VOL.

Wine List

Dry: Seyval Blanc, Vidal Blanc, Chambourcin, Valley Red (red hybrid blend)

Semidry: Belle of Donegal (white hybrids such as Aurore, Seyval, and Vidal), Classic White (white hybrid blend), Vignoles, Candlelight (white hybrids and a little red wine for color), Naughty Marietta (red hybrid blend), Montmorency Cherry

Semisweet: Bainbridge White (Vidal and other white hybrids), Whisper White (blend of white hybrid grapes), Bainbridge Rosé (white hybrids such as Aurore and Vidal, plus red wine for color), Bainbridge Red (DeChaunac and other red hybrids), Apple

Sweet: Niagara, Fantasy (Concord, Niagara and other native American grapes), Spicy Red (Concord plus natural spices), Concord, Country Cherry, Black Raspberry

Best-selling Wines: Candlelight, Fantasy

Hours

Monday–Saturday, 10:00 A.M. to 5:00 P.M.; Sunday, 1:00 to 4:00 P.M. (Closed Easter Sunday, Thanksgiving, Christmas, and New Year's Day.)

Services and Events

Self-guided vineyard and winery tours, patios and lawn for picnics, creek and woodlands for walks, lawn concerts featuring big bands and small light-rock groups on Saturday evenings in July and August.

Directions

The winery is located in western Lancaster County, not far from the Susquehanna River. From Lancaster or York, take Route 30 to the Columbia exit, and go north on Route 441 for 8 miles. Watch for the Nissley Winery sign, and turn right on Wickersham Road. Follow the winery signs for 1½ miles to the winery.

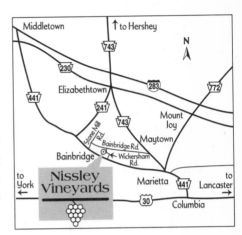

Extensions

- Nissley Wine Shop at Capital City Mall, Capital Mall Dr., Camp Hill, (717) 737-7844.
- Nissley Wine Shop at Colonial Park, Route 22 and Colonial Road, Harrisburg, (717) 541-1004.
- Nissley Wine Shop at Park City Center, Route 30 and Harrisburg Pike, Lancaster, (717) 392-6055.
- Nissley Wine Shop at Rockvale Square, Routes 30 East and 896, Lancaster, (717) 299-5101.

🍇 Oak Spring Winery

R.D. 1, Box 612, Altoona, PA 16601
PHONE: (814) 946-3799
FAX: (814) 946-4245
E-MAIL: oakspring@keyconn.net
WEBSITE: www.oakspringwinery.com

LOCATION: **Mountains, Central Area**

WHEN SYLVIA AND JOHN SCHRAFF FIRST BEGAN TO PLAN A WINERY, THEY figured they would grow some grapes on a hillside, convert an old garage into a winery on the first floor, create an apartment upstairs, and put a tasting room down near the road. About halfway up the drive, an oak tree grew at the spot where a spring came out of the ground and created a marshy area full of cattails. That tree inspired the name Oak Spring and became the symbol for the winery that still appears on their labels. However, before this version of the Schraffs' winery dream could come true, the farm adjoining their property came up for sale. The Schraffs bought the 57-acre farm, complete with a barn that could be used for winemaking and a small house that would serve as a tasting room.

The Schraffs planted 3 acres of vineyard and in September 1987 received their license to open a winery. By November they decided that they should open the winery to take advantage of the Christmas season. That turned out to be a wise decision, as the holiday season is a major time for wine sales in their area.

When they opened the winery, both John and Sylvia had other jobs. Sylvia was president and chief executive officer of Home Nursing Agency, and John, initially involved in city planning, in 1990 became executive director of the Altoona–Blair County Chamber of Commerce. Neither one had time to devote to developing the winery business, and after three years, they hired a winemaker to help them out. That worked for several years, until the winemaker left. At that point the winery was at a crossroads, and several things happened almost simultaneously that allowed the Schraffs not only to remain in the wine business, but to grow and expand.

First, a building along the main north-south highway from Altoona became available. Originally a fruit farm market, the structure had about 7,500 square feet of space, enough for a winemaking facility, case storage, a cold room for wine stabilization, an adequate tasting room, and extra space for winemaking or beer-brewing classes. Shortly after this building became available, John's son Scott decided he'd like to return to Altoona and begin to learn the wine business. Five years later, Scott is running the winery, and John and Sylvia have retired from their full-time jobs and from day-to-day responsibilities at the winery. Sylvia still helps with the winemaking, and John assists in the marketing area. Scott is assisted by John Hoover as manager of sales, and today the winery is producing approximately 15,000 gallons of wine.

The Schraffs currently have about 3 acres of producing vineyards, which yield approximately 10 percent of the winery's grapes. The remainder are purchased from Erie County and other vineyards.

This carefully restored and decorated old carriage is one of two used in the tasting room at Oak Spring Winery to display the wines.

The winery is enthusiastically supported by the local population. Businesses and local people consider Oak Spring to be "their" winery and anticipate that Oak Spring wines will be served at various local events. The Schraffs developed a series of wine labels that cater to the local area, and specifically to the railroading tradition of Altoona. Three semisweet wines, K4, 1361, and Horseshoe Curve, have railroad themes, and the price of each bottle includes a donation to the local Railroad Museum.

At Oak Spring Winery, the tasting room features a wide range of wine-related accessories. Sylvia has always enjoyed making beer, and the winery also has supplies and holds classes for both home winemakers and home beer brewers. Scott has recently added a club for brewers.

Wine List

Dry: Vidal Blanc, Vidal Blanc Reserve, Chambourcin, Chardonnay

Semidry: White 'Cin (Chambourcin and Vidal), Cayuga White, Red Caboose (DeChaunac), Candlelite (Vidal), Riesling

Semisweet: Niagara, Steuben, Pink Catawba, Concord, Harvest Red (Baco Noir), Holiday (mostly Concord, plus spices), K4 (Concord), 1361 (Catawba), Horseshoe Curve (Vidal, Cayuga, and Chambourcin)

Sweet: Peach, Apple, Spiced Apple, Berry Berry (Strawberry and Raspberry), Classic Cherry (Montmorency cherries)

Best-selling Wines: White 'Cin, Steuben

Hours

Daily, 11:00 A.M. to 6:00 P.M.

Services and Events

Custom wine labels, large room for special events or parties, extensive gift shop, home winemaking and brewing supplies and classes, and a brewers' club.

Directions

Take the Pinecroft exit from I-99/Route 220. Head west on Route 764 to the first traffic light, and turn right on Old Route 220. The winery is on the right in about 1/2 mile. There is excellent signage directing visitors to the winery, including one of the largest on-highway state signs we've ever seen.

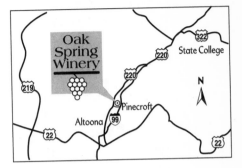

Extensions

Galleria Mall, off Route 219, Johnstown.

# Oregon Hill Winery

840 Oregon Hill Rd., Morris, PA 16938
PHONE: (570) 353-2711

LOCATION: **Mountains, Central Area**

OREGON HILL WINERY IS NOT EASY TO FIND. IT'S LOCATED CLOSE TO THE New York State border north of Williamsport in the central part of the state, where there are not many people, and there are few signs to let you know where it is. The winery doesn't need signs, however—it's located in the middle of a resort area where 80 percent of the property is owned by people who live somewhere else, primarily Reading, Lancaster, Philadelphia, or New Jersey. These second-home owners come to the area on weekends, in the summer, and for hunting and fishing seasons. When they arrive, they buy wine by the case. The community even has a small airstrip for private planes.

For many wineries, the busiest sales days are close to holidays or between Thanksgiving and Christmas. At Oregon Hill, however, the peak sales days are the days before the opening of bear season and trout season. Their customers are very loyal; one man even flew his helicopter from Delaware, landed on the road in front of the winery, came into the winery for a case of Cabernet Sauvignon, and then immediately flew back home!

The story of Oregon Hill Winery began when Alfred Swendrowski moved his family to the area in the early 1970s. He bought the Idlewood Inn, an eight-seat bar, and converted it into an Alpine-style restaurant. He also bought a 100-acre farm. Al was a home winemaker and, in the course of looking for grapes and wine in the area, became friends with Dr. Konstantin Frank in New York State. Dr. Frank is a well-known viticultural pioneer who planted and grew vinifera grapes successfully in New York State and persuaded many other people to try to grow vinifera as well. Al decided he wanted to grow Cabernet Sauvignon, Chardonnay, and Gewürztraminer on his farm, even though Dr. Frank was skeptical that Al could be successful in that location. The winters are cold and long in northern Pennsylvania, and after six years, only some of the Cabernet Sauvignon vines were still alive. Today, one grape post on the edge of the meadow is all that remains of the vineyard.

Alfred Swendrowski had planted the vineyard because he wanted to start an estate winery, one that grew the grapes used to make the wine. The weather defeated the vineyard project, and state regulations came close to defeating his goal of establishing a winery. He applied for a winery license, but because he had a liquor license for his restaurant, he was not eligible for a winery license, according to the laws in Pennsylvania. Consequently, his son Eric, then eighteen years old, took over the idea of starting a winery. In order to do so, Eric had to purchase the barn from his parents and set up a separate business. He applied for his winery license in 1983 and opened in 1985 as probably the youngest winery owner in Pennsylvania. His parents continued to run the restaurant until Al retired in 1996, and both help in the winery when needed.

The winery has grown from 1,000 to 6,000 gallons per year. Because he cannot grow his own grapes, Eric purchases fruit from Erie County

Eric Swendrowski stands behind the tasting bar stocked with bottles of the wines available for tasting and sale at Oregon Hill Winery.

and also from local growers with better microclimates. He gets the Concord grapes for his Canyon Country Concord from a vineyard that's not far from the Grand Canyon of Pennsylvania, a tourist attraction outside Wellsboro, 17 miles north of the winery. Apples and peaches come from an orchard near Pottsville.

Al's latest project was to develop some of the acreage of the farm into a nine-hole golf course. There's a small ski resort down the road from the winery, and the golf course provides another activity for vacationers during the summer. In winter, the golf course is an excellent place to cross-country ski.

The winery is in the ground floor of what had been a working farm barn until the Swendrowskis bought it. The tasting room is located in one of the old bull pens; adjoining are two other bull pens, which Eric plans to use either for case storage or to expand the tasting room.

Oregon Hill

1998

Mountain Raspberry

Pennsylvania Raspberry Table Wine
Produced and Bottled by Oregon Hill Wine Co. Inc.
Morris, PA 16938 (570) 353-2711
contains sulfites

GOVERNMENT WARNING: (1) ACCORDING TO THE SURGEON GENERAL, WOMEN SHOULD NOT DRINK ALCOHOLIC BEVERAGES DURING PREGNANCY BECAUSE OF THE RISK OF BIRTH DEFECTS. (2) CONSUMPTION OF ALCOHOLIC BEVERAGES IMPAIRS YOUR ABILITY TO DRIVE A CAR OR OPERATE MACHINERY, AND MAY CAUSE HEALTH PROBLEMS.

Wine List

Dry: Chardonnay, Cabernet Sauvignon, Reserve (DeChaunac and Foch), Pinot Noir

Semidry: Riesling, Seyval Blanc, Baco Noir

Semisweet: Sussbeeren Tropfchen (some vintages Riesling; other vintages Vidal), Mountain White (Niagara), Mountain Red (Concord), Mountain Laurel Blush (Catawba, Aurore, and Delaware), Rosen Cavalier (Vidal, Seyval, and Aurore; sometimes Ravat [Vignoles])

Sweet: Canyon Country Concord, Mountain Apple, Mountain Peach, Mountain Cherry, Mountain Raspberry, Mountain Blueberry, Spiced Apple

Best-selling Wine: Mountain Red

Hours

Daily, 10:00 A.M. to 5:30 P.M.

Services and Events

Public nine-hole golf course.

Directions

From Williamsport: Go west on Route 220 to Route 287 and head north. Approximately 7 miles after driving through the small town of English Center, watch for signs for Ski Sawmill and also the Pine Marsh Golf Course, both of which are in the hamlet of Oregon Hill. Turn left on Oregon Hill Road immediately after the Inn 287; the winery is on the right in about 1/2 mile. If you come to the Idlewood Restaurant on the left, you have gone too far.

From Wellsboro: The winery is about 17 miles south of Wellsboro. Take Route 287 south; after passing through the small town of Morris, watch for the Idlewood Restaurant on the right. Shortly thereafter, turn right onto Oregon Hill Road. The winery is on the right in about 1/2 mile.

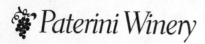 *Paterini Winery*

21 Hemlock St., Ellsworth, PA 15331
PHONE: (724) 239-4656

LOCATION: **Mountains, Southwest Area**

AL PATERINI WORKED FOR THIRTY-FIVE YEARS AS A STEELWORKER AND A coal miner, and when he retired, he started a third career as a winemaker and opened the Paterini Winery in 1996. The winery is one of the smallest in Pennsylvania and is not easily located. There are no large signs along a highway to guide you, and the newspaper for the Pennsylvania Wine Association, *The Pennsylvania Wine Traveler*, does not list the winery or give directions on how to find it. The winery does exist, however, in the little town of Ellsworth south of Pittsburgh. Al's friends and neighbors know where he is and stop in regularly to see if Al has gotten around to bottling more of their favorite wines.

Al is the owner, winemaker, tasting room manager, and sales clerk. He produces and sells less than 1,000 gallons of wine per year, all in the basement of his home. The basement door opens into an entryway that now serves as the winery's tasting room. There is just enough space for Al to pour samples of wine while standing behind a small table, but if more than three people come in, one of them must stand in the doorway.

The winery is the width of the house and has room for some small stainless steel tanks, a few plastic drums, a collection of 15-gallon stainless steel kegs, and some carboys. It's not a facility where tall people would be comfortable working, as the ceiling is only about 5 1/2 feet high. But Al is not that tall, and to him, the winery is his little piece of heaven. Though he has no plans to increase production, he is working on ways to make winemaking a little easier within the space he has, such as expanding his deck outside, putting in a small crush pad, and adding a chute similar to a coal chute to deliver red grapes from the pad outside directly into the fermentation area. He also has designs for converting the laundry room area into a case storage area or to expand the tasting room.

Al has a few grapevines growing over an arbor in his backyard and about 1/4 acre of grapes planted on a cousin's farm. For the most part, he purchases fruit from Erie County.

Wine List

Dry: Chardonnay, Cabernet Sauvignon, Cabernet Franc, DeChaunac, Red's Special (Cabernet, DeChaunac, Chancellor, and Chambourcin)

Semidry: Autumn Blush (Niagara, Delaware, Catawba, and Blackberry), Niagara Blush, Seyval Blanc, and Reena's Rosé

Sweet: Delaware, Strawberry, Concord, Blackberry

Al Paterini has one of Pennsylvania's smallest wineries in the basement of his home outside of Pittsburgh.

Best-selling Wines: Autumn Blush, Red's Special

Hours

Open Monday–Saturday by chance or appointment. Closed Sunday and holidays.

Services and Events

Gift baskets.

Directions

Paterini Winery is south of Pittsburgh and east of Washington. From the north, take Route 917 south to Ellsworth. Turn right onto Beech Street, then right into the alley (there is a small sign indicating you are in the right place). The winery is on the left. From the south, take Route 917 north from Route 40; go about 5 miles into Ellsworth, and turn left on Beech Street, then right into the alley.

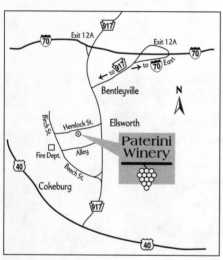

🍇 Peace Valley Winery

P.O. Box 94, 300 Old Limekiln Rd., Chalfont, PA 18914
PHONE: (215) 249-9058
E-MAIL: peacevalwinery@enter.com

LOCATION: Southeast, Philadelphia Area

MANY WINERY OWNERS WILL TELL YOU THAT THEIR INSPIRATION FOR START-
ing a winery came from a trip to France. Susan Gross, who opened Peace
Valley Winery in 1984, traveled to France twenty years earlier, while
working for an agricultural chemical company, and came back wanting
to grow not grapes, but dwarf espaliered apple trees like the ones she saw
growing on trellises in Paris gardens. The first step was to find an appropriate farm. Her first break was finding a real estate agent who was an
amateur horticulturist. After a year's search, Susan found a piece of land
in Bucks County with old apple trees on it that were still producing after
a bad frost had killed most of the fruit blossoms in other local orchards.

The second step was to find a source of dwarf fruit trees. No one in
Bucks County was growing dwarf or espaliered apple trees. By 1971
Susan located a dwarf tree association, but by then she had become interested in grapes as well. Though the growing conditions for apples and
grapes are different, both orchards and vineyards use much of the same
equipment, which makes the two fairly compatible. She visited Mel Gor-
don, the original owner of Conestoga Vineyards in Birchrunville, Pennsylvania; learned about Philip Wagner, owner of Boordy Nursery in
Maryland; visited Doug Moorhead at Presque Isle Wine Cellars in North
East, Pennsylvania; and met George Remailly, a viticulturist at the New
York State Agricultural Experiment Station in Geneva, New York, who
was originally from Bucks County and had a large collection of hybrid
grape varieties. She planted her first grapes in 1968 and gradually accumulated a wide variety of experimental grapes from the research stations
in Vineland, Ontario and Geneva and other people who learned of her
interest in different, unusual varieties. Over the years, Susan has tested
over two hundred different varieties of grapes.

In the late 1970s Susan was running a pick-your-own fruit operation
for both apples and grapes. She sold grapes to amateur winemakers and

Susan Gross pours samples of her wines at Peace Valley Vineyards.

experimented with making wine. About that time she found out that the company she worked for was contemplating moving out of the area. Knowing that she didn't want to leave her farm, Susan began to prepare for the day her company left Pennsylvania. She revamped her vineyard, pulling out and replanting varieties with the goal of opening a winery. The company moved in 1981; by 1983 she built her winery building, and she officially opened the winery in 1984 with her partner, Rob Kolmus.

Today both the winery and the vineyards have expanded. Susan's original farm had 24 acres; she and Rob have since purchased an additional 12 acres. While there are still 4 acres in dwarf apple trees, Susan and Rob plan to replace one of those acres with grapes. They plan to add more Carmine and Traminette and would like to expand their Chardonnay, Cabernet, Merlot, and Chambourcin plantings.

The winery now makes between 8,000 and 10,000 gallons of wine each year. "We make country wines," Susan says, meaning wines that often are blends of different grape varieties but end up being wines that people like to drink. Some of the wines at Peace Valley are vinifera wines, such as Chardonnay and Cabernet, but both Susan and Rob are hesitant to expand their vinifera wines. They would prefer to have their wines, and Pennsylvania's wines in general, become known for being good, well-made wines, without necessarily being from vinifera grapes. As Susan says, Pennsylvania has proved that vinifera grapes can be grown here, but enough problems remain with those varieties that she does not want to expand the vinifera acreage much beyond 25 percent of the total vineyard.

Currently all Peace Valley wines are sold at the winery. Susan and Rob recognize that when their new vineyards begin to produce a crop, they will need to expand their markets. They have had extensions of the winery in the past and will probably do so in the future.

Four of the sweet wines and two other wines on the wine list are seasonal, including Nouveau, released the weekend before Thanksgiving;

Spring Fling, released in mid-April; Summer Solstice, which becomes available on June 20; and Winter Solstice, released in mid-December.

Wine List

Dry: Seyval, Chardonnay Reserve, Bucks Blush, Cabernet Sauvignon, Excalibur, New Britain Red, Nouveau

Semidry: New Britain White (Siegfried and Cayuga), New Britain Rosé, Spring Fling

Semisweet: Chalfont Rouge

Sweet: Niagara, Fredonia, Blushing Apple, Nectarine, Summer Solstice, Winter Solstice (Cherry), Spiced Apple, Spicewine

Sparkling: Champagne (Ventura), Spumante

Best-selling Wine: New Britain White

Hours

January 1–Thanksgiving, Wednesday–Sunday, noon to 6:00 P.M.; Saturday, 10:00 A.M. to 6:00 P.M. Thanksgiving–December 31, Monday–Thursday, 10:00 A.M. to 6:00 P.M.; Friday and Saturday, 10:00 A.M. to 8:00 P.M.; Sunday, noon to 6:00 P.M.

Services and Events

Specialty labels.

Directions

From Doylestown, go north on Route 611 to Route 313. Head northwest on Route 313, and turn left onto New Galena Road. In about 2 miles, as you pass Lake Galena, the road bears to the right and becomes Old Limekiln Road. Go 1 mile, and the winery is on the left.

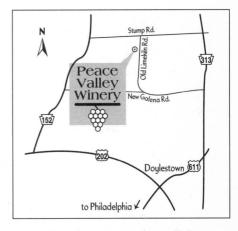

Note: If you are heading south on Route 611, there is no exit off the bypass for Route 313. You must either take Business Route 611 or go one exit past Route 313 and take the next exit, turn around, and go north on the bypass to Route 313.

🍇 Penn Shore Vineyards

10225 E. Lake Rd. (Route 5), North East, PA 16428
PHONE: (814) 725-8688
FAX: (814) 725-9422
WEBSITE: www.pennshore.com

LOCATION: Lake Erie
(Lake Erie Quality Wine Alliance)

ONE OF THE FIRST WINERIES TO OPEN AFTER THE PASSAGE OF THE LIMITED Winery Act in 1968 was Penn Shore Vineyards in North East. Three growers, Blair McCord, George Luke, and George Sceiford, set up a corporation, obtained one of the first two limited winery licenses, and formally opened their winery on April 30, 1970, with a reception for the Erie County press corps. In the first year, the winery produced 50,000 gallons. The wines were sold through the State Store system as well as at the winery.

In the 1970s the winery became one of the largest in the state, with a storage capacity of 175,000 gallons, although actual production was 45,000 to 50,000 gallons. The partners, however, discovered that it was much easier to make wine than to sell it. Then, as the result of litigation on harassment charges against a former Penn Shore manager, the winery went into bankruptcy in 1989. The United States District Court approved a reorganization plan in 1990 that allowed Robert Mazza and two shareholders of Penn Shore Vineyards to buy the winery building and real estate. During the period of bankruptcy, the winery was operated by Bob Mazza under a court-approved management contract that had a provision allowing him to obtain a controlling interest in the winery. Since then, Mazza Vineyards and Penn Shore Vineyards have been operated as two separate corporations by Bob Mazza. Penn Shore Vineyards remains a full-production facility, although the grapes are pressed at Mazza Vineyards before being trucked to Penn Shore. Currently the winery produces about 15,000 gallons a year. The winery purchases most of the fruit used for its wines. Penn Shore has 2 acres of Concord grapes and no plans to add more vineyards. When Bob Mazza took over Penn Shore, he did so with the intention of maintaining its traditional line of wines, which it continues to sell today.

Wine List

Dry: Chardonnay, Seyval Blanc, Vignoles, Baco Noir, Dry Red

Semidry: Vidal Blanc, Chablis (Seyval and Cayuga), Bianca (Cayuga and Vidal), Burgundy (Baco Noir, DeChaunac and Landot)

Semisweet: Blush (primarily Steuben), Kir (Seyval and Catawba, with black current flavoring), Diamond, Lambruscano (Concord and DeChaunac)

Sweet: Niagara, Concord, Holiday Spice, Pink Catawba, Crystal Lake White (Vidal, Cayuga and Vignoles)

Penn Shore Vineyards is the only winery in Erie County where a visitor can see the vineyards, the winery buildings, and Lake Erie in the background (above the vines at the left).

Sparkling: Champagne (extra dry)

Best-selling Wine: Kir

Hours

July–August, Monday–Saturday, 9:00 A.M. to 8:00 P.M.; Sunday, 11:00 A.M. to 5:00 P.M.; September–June, Monday–Saturday, 9:00 A.M. to 5:30 P.M.; Sunday, 11:00 A.M. to 5:00 P.M.

Directions

From I-90 east of Erie, take exit 11. Go north on Route 89 through the town of North East, and turn left on Route 5. Penn Shore Winery is on the left in 1 mile.

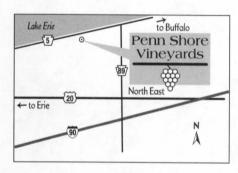

Extension

Naturally Yours Gourmet Foods & Gifts, 3741 W. 26th St., Erie, a joint outlet with Mazza Vineyards and Presque Isle Wine Cellars, (814) 835-5255 (open Monday–Friday, 10:00 A.M. to 8:30 P.M.; Saturday, 10:00 A.M. to 4:00 P.M.; Sunday, noon to 4:00 P.M.).

Philadelphia Wine Company

3061 Miller St., Philadelphia, PA 19134
PHONE: (215) 425-4144

LOCATION: **Southeast, Philadelphia Area**

SOME WINERIES ARE NATIONAL IN ORIENTATION, SOME ARE REGIONAL, AND some are local. Another category is the city winery, which occurs infrequently in the East and only occasionally on the West Coast in places like San Francisco, Oakland, and Los Angeles. The Philadelphia Wine Company falls into this category. It is a neighborhood winery with twenty-three thousand potential customers, all within walking distance. Locals know that the winery is housed in the old icehouse on Miller Street, and owner Tom Kelly has sold out of wine each year by attracting customers from his Philadelphia neighborhood. The winery facility is in one part of the old warehouse, and the tasting room is in the combination office and storage room.

The wines reflect the neighborhood orientation of the winery. Each wine has a proprietary name that has meaning for local people. The winery is in the Port Richmond area of Philadelphia, so two wines are Port Richmond Red and Port Richmond White. The images used on the labels are local landmarks: A well-known Indian statue from a neighborhood park appears on the Wissahickon Valley wines; the icehouse sign illustrates the Port Richmond Red and the Port Richmond White; the boathouses for rowing sculls along the Schuylkill River appear on the Boathouse Red Wine.

Tom Kelly grew up in the Roxborough neighborhood of Philadelphia and has operated his catering business from the same building in the Port Richmond area for twenty years. In 1992 he started to make wine as an amateur and in 1996 he opened the winery. His goal is to make well-made, simple, and affordable wines that his neighbors who are working people will like. Using proprietary wine names on his labels has allowed Tom to blend grapes to create balanced wines from whatever grapes are available during a given harvest. Though the blend may not be exactly

The Philadelphia Wine Company is located in a former icehouse. On the right are some of the row houses in the neighborhood where more than 23,000 people live within walking distance of the winery.

the same from one year to the next, the style of a certain wine stays the same—and the wines taste good.

Tom would like to increase production to 10,000 gallons in the next two or three years. The icehouse has plenty of space, and he could probably produce as much as 100,000 gallons. However, the size of the winery will depend on the availability of grapes and on the continued and increasing support of his neighborhood customers. He plans to add Fishtown Red and White wines (named for another Philadelphia neighborhood), in larger bottles with screw caps to increase their user-friendliness, and 12-ounce bottles of a hard cider called Big Scrapple's Apple (named for a popular breakfast meat found in southeastern Pennsylvania).

The Philadelphia Wine Company is a city winery and currently has no vineyards. Tom once said that he would never grow grapes, but as good-quality grapes have become more difficult to obtain, he is reevaluating that statement and considering different options. He is now trying to develop contacts that might lead to fruit farmers expanding their crops to include grapes grown to his specifications.

Wine List

Dry: Wissahickon Valley White (Vidal and Seyval), Wissahickon Valley Red (DeChaunac, Chancellor, and Chambourcin), Boathouse Red (Chambourcin, DeChaunac, and Chancellor)

PHILADELPHIA
WINE CO.

Boathouse Red
Table Wine

Produced and bottled by Tommy Kelly - Caterer, Inc.
Philadelphia, PA. 19134

Slightly sweet: Port Richmond White (Vidal and Seyval), Port Richmond Red

Semisweet: Icehouse Crimson (Chancellor, Vidal, and Seyval) Appleation Port Richmond (Apple)

Best-selling Wine: Icehouse Crimson

Hours

By chance or by appointment.

Directions

The Philadelphia Wine Company is located north of the Benjamin Franklin Bridge not far from the Delaware River in the Port Richmond neighborhood of Philadelphia.

From I-95 North: Exit at Allegheny Avenue, and turn left at the end of the exit ramp. Turn left at the first light onto Richmond Street, then right onto Allegheny Avenue. Go several blocks to Belgrade Avenue and turn left. At Clearfield Street, turn right, then turn left at the first intersection onto Miller Street (this is immediately after passing the Rizzo Police Athletic League Building). The winery is in the red brick warehouse building that is almost straight ahead of you, where Miller Street jogs slightly to the right at the end of the first block. Just below the top of the building are words identifying the original ownership: "Kensington Hygeia Ice Co., Richmond Station."

From I-95 South: Exit at Allegheny Avenue, and turn right at the end of the exit ramp. Turn left at the first light onto Richmond Street, and follow the directions above.

Note: When we visited the winery, Miller Street was not labeled at the intersection with Clearfield Street; it is a narrow, one-way street lined with parked cars.

🍇 Pinnacle Ridge Winery

407 Old Route 22, Kutztown, PA 19530
PHONE: (610) 756-4481
FAX: (610) 756-6385
E-MAIL: Pinridge@aol.com

LOCATION: Southeast, Lehigh Valley
(Lehigh Valley Wine Trail)

MOST WINERIES BEGIN BY MAKING TABLE WINES AND THEN DECIDE TO diversify their product line by adding a sparkling wine. At Pinnacle Ridge, Brad and Dawn Knapp set out to become Pennsylvania's sparkling wine winery first and foremost, but like many in the wine business, they found that what they would like to make has to be tempered by what the customers want. As a result, Pinnacle Ridge also makes a number of dry and semidry table wines. Today sparkling wine makes up about 25 percent of their production, all of it made in the traditional French *méthode champenoise* manner. The Knapps produce three sparkling wines: a dry Brut, a slightly sweet Blanc de Blanc that is made from Cayuga; and a Brut Reserve that is a blend of traditional Champagne grapes—Pinot Noir, Meunier, and Chardonnay.

Brad Knapp did not initially plan to become a winemaker. While he was working on his Ph.D. in chemistry at the University of Wisconsin, he started to make beer, and then a friend got him interested in making wine as well. After graduation, he took a job in Pennsylvania, and he and his wife, Dawn, set out to find a location that would meet their requirements for a vineyard and winery. After a year's search, they found a farm west of Allentown with a southern exposure, a historic house, a Pennsylvania bank barn built in 1851, and a good location less than a mile from an exit of a four-lane highway. They purchased the farm in 1990, planted 3 acres of vineyard, and opened the winery in 1995.

In October 1998 Brad left his job as director of technology at Diamonex to become a consultant and to put more time into the vineyard and winery. Dawn runs the business end of the winery and helps in the tasting room, and Brad does everything else. The bank barn has been converted from a dairy to a winery that takes advantage of the different levels offered by a barn built into a hill. The grapes are crushed in an upstairs room and then gravity-fed by hose into tanks on a level below. The area that once housed cows now contains stainless steel wine tanks, barrels rest in the feeding troughs, and an adjacent room serves as the tasting area. The old potato cellar, also built into the hill, serves as the sparkling wine facility and contains ten French riddling racks full of champagne bottles waiting for colder weather so that the sparkling wine can be disgorged and finished.

Three acres near the barn have been planted with Pinot Noir, Chardonnay, Chambourcin, and Vignoles. While the Knapps do not have any additional land to plant at the winery site, a friend not far away has a 7-acre vineyard containing Cayuga, Vidal, Chardonnay, Pinot Noir, and 2 acres of Chambourcin. That farm has an additional 200 acres available, and the owners and Brad are in the process of deciding what kinds of grapes would be best to grow on the site.

Brad and Dawn Knapp located the tasting room for Pinnacle Ridge Winery in a corner room of their Pennsylvania bank barn that was built over 100 years ago.

Wine List

Dry: Chardonnay, Vidal Blanc, Chambourcin, Pinot Noir

Slightly Sweet: Chambourcin Rosé, Vidal Blanc

Sweet: Cayuga White, Sweet Seduction

Sparkling: Brut (Vidal and Chambourcin), Brut Reserve (Pinot Noir, Pinot Meunier, and Chardonnay), Blanc de Blanc (Cayuga)

Best-selling Wine: Vidal Blanc

Hours

Saturday, 10:00 A.M. to 5:00 P.M.; Sunday, noon to 5:00 P.M. (Other hours by appointment.)

Directions

Take Route 22/78 from Allentown to exit 12 for Krumsville and Route 737. Go north on Route 737 to the blinking light in Krumsville. Turn right onto Old Route 22. Pinnacle Ridge Winery is located 0.8 mile ahead on the left.

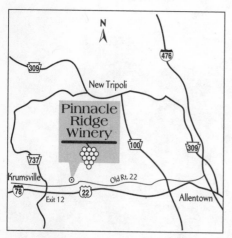

🍇 Presque Isle Wine Cellars

9440 Buffalo Rd., North East, PA 16428
PHONE: (814) 725-1314, (800) 488-7492
FAX: (814) 725-2092
E-MAIL: prwc@erie.net
WEBSITE: www.erie.net/~prwc

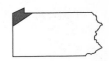

LOCATION: Lake Erie area
(Lake Erie Quality Wine Alliance)

NOT LONG AFTER HE RETURNED FROM SERVING IN THE U.S. ARMY IN GERmany in the 1950s and started to help his father on the family grape farm, Doug Moorhead met Bill Konnerth, a home winemaker who suggested that Doug plant some wine grapes. Philip Wagner, who ran Boordy Nursery in Maryland, recommended some French hybrids, and Dr. Konstantin Frank in New York suggested planting some vinifera. Soon the vineyard began to supply Doug and Bill with grapes to make into wine. In 1960 they started the Lake Erie Wine Club. The members found it difficult to locate the equipment and supplies they needed, so Bill and Doug began to import winemaking equipment and supplies. This led to the opening of Presque Isle Wine Cellars in North East on February 17, 1964, not as a winery, but as a source of juice and winery supplies for home winemakers.

During the 1960s Doug worked with several other growers in the Erie area and from the southeastern part of Pennsylvania to get the laws in the state changed to allow farm wineries. In 1968 the Limited Winery Act was passed, permitting wineries to make up to 50,000 gallons of wine from Pennsylvania fruit and to sell that wine at the farm. Presque Isle and Penn Shore Vineyards were the first two wineries to be licensed; both made wine in the fall of 1969 and opened their wineries in the spring of 1970.

Bill Konnerth retired in 1975, and the current owners of Presque Isle Wine Cellars are Doug and his wife, Marlene, and Marlene's brother and sister-in-law, Marc and Lori Boettcher. Today Presque Isle continues to sell winemaking supplies and equipment for home winemakers and small wineries and supplies many thousands of gallons of juice to both amateur and professional winemakers. The winery remains a small part

Marlene and Doug Moorhead opened one of the first wineries in Pennsylvania after Doug and several others were successful in passing the legislation permitting limited wineries in the state.

of the overall business, usually making about 7,000 to 8,000 gallons of wine per year. In 1998, however, because of a bumper crop of grapes, the winery produced 16,000 gallons. Presque Isle's winemaker, Bob Greene, says he has "wine in tanks, wine in barrels, wine sitting out in the woods. It's going to be a challenge to get it all taken care of properly!"

Presque Isle has no vineyards under its own ownership, but Moorhead Vineyards, Inc., operated by Doug, has over 165 acres planted, of which 35 acres are wine grapes that go to Presque Isle. The first vinifera were planted in 1958 after Doug had met Dr. Frank and Charles Fournier at Gold Seal Winery in New York. At one time, Doug had over two hundred different varieties of all types under test but that number has been reduced to fewer than thirty. It has taken years of experimenting in both the vineyard and the winery for Doug to determine that Riesling and Cabernet Franc are the best vinifera for his site, and Vidal and Chambourcin the best hybrids. In the near future, he would like to plant more vinifera as well as some Traminette and Chambourcin. Eventually,

Doug would like to let Marc and Lori take over the winery end of the business and spend more time in his vineyard.

Presque Isle Wine Cellars makes a wide variety of wines, with some lots in small, experimental batches. The experimental winemaking research supports the winery's grape and juice sales to amateurs and helps the winery improve the quality of its wine. Doug thinks production will probably increase to 10,000 gallons on a yearly basis. Presque Isle plans to put up a new building in the spring of 2000 and have it finished before harvest. The goal is to relieve some of crowding in the wine- and juice-processing areas.

The tasting room offers wine accessories for sale as well as an extensive selection of books on growing grapes, making wine, the wine industry, and appreciating wine.

Barrels, stainless steel kegs, and glass carboys at Presque Isle Wine Cellars.

Wine List

Dry: Seyval Blanc, Chardonnay, Lemberger, Chambourcin, Cabernet Franc, Cabernet Sauvignon, Merlot

Semidry: Reflections of Lake Erie (vinifera-hybrid blend), Vignoles, Riesling, Rosé (Pinot Noir and Chardonnay)

Semisweet: Muscat Ottonel

Sweet: Creekside White (Catawba and Delaware), Creekside Blush (Steuben and Fredonia), Creekside Red (primarily Fredonia)

Best-selling Wine: Chardonnay

Hours

Monday–Saturday, 8:00 A.M. to 6:00 P.M. (Closed on Sundays and legal holidays.) Extended hours during harvest, usually mid-September through October, Monday–Saturday, 8:00 A.M. to 6:30 P.M.; Sunday, 8:00 A.M. to 3:00 P.M.

Services and Events

Custom labeling.

Directions

Take exit 11 off I-90 east of Erie. Go north toward Lake Erie on Route 89. Turn left on Route 20 in the town of North East. Go 3½ miles west; there is a cemetery on the left, and the winery is on the right.

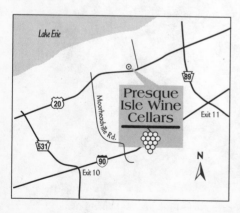

Extension

Naturally Yours Gourmet Foods & Gifts, 3741 W. 26th St., Erie, a joint outlet with Mazza Vineyards and Penn Shore Vineyards, (814) 835-5255 (open Monday–Friday, 10:00 A.M. to 8:30 P.M.; Saturday, 10:00 A.M. to 4:00 P.M.; Sunday, noon to 4:00 P.M.).

Quaker Ridge Winery

211 S. Wade Ave., Washington, PA 15301
PHONE: (724) 222-2914

LOCATION: Mountains, Southwest Area

IN 1988 JOHN JACOBS, A PROFESSOR AT WASHINGTON AND JEFFERSON COL-
lege, started Quaker Ridge Winery after he received a grant to do a study
on the uses of different kinds of fruit in western Pennsylvania. The fruit
for his study was grown south of the town of Washington on a farm that
was first owned by John England, a Quaker who was ultimately buried in
the cemetery on a ridge near his farm. The winery was given the name
Quaker Ridge because of this association with the farm, although the
winery itself has never been located there. Instead, John Jacobs located
the winery in a 120-year-old house just outside the downtown area of
Washington. The main room, now the tasting room, previously was a
mom-and-pop grocery store, and the wine cellar in the basement was a
butcher shop.

John hired a manager to run the winery, as he was more interested in
fruit experiments than in making and selling wine. After two years, it
became apparent that the manager was not doing the job, so John put the
winery up for sale. In 1990 Bill and Barbara Verscharen purchased the
winery, as Bill liked the idea of making and selling wine as a hobby. Bill
had worked in construction, but a back injury ended that career. Because
of his limitations, Bill buys his grapes from the Lake Erie area and hires
younger people to help with the heavy, hard-work aspects of making
wine. Since he took over the winery, Bill has increased production from
300 or 400 to 3,500 gallons, the maximum that the basement wine cellar
can handle. Currently Bill is working with a young couple that has an
interest in making wine and might possibly be interested in expanding
the winery's operation and participating in its continued growth.

Bill Verscharen (left) and two of his staff from Quaker Ridge Winery tasted wine together at the meeting of the Pennsylvania Wine Association at State College in April 1999.

Wine List

Dry: Chianti (Baco Noir and DeChaunac)

Semidry: Chablis (Vidal and Seyval), Niagara, Burgundy (Baco Noir and DeChaunac)

Semisweet: Concord, Blush (White Zinfandel-style; Seyval, Vidal, and 15 percent Concord), Vintage Red (Baco Noir and DeChaunac), Sauterne (Vidal, and Seyval)

Sweet: Spicy Apple (Jonathan apples), Country Plum, Almond (Chablis plus natural almond flavoring), Raspberry (Concord and DeChaunac plus raspberry flavoring)

Best-selling Wine: Blush

Hours

Thursday and Friday, 11:00 A.M. to 6:00 P.M.; Saturday and Sunday, noon to 5:00 P.M. (Other hours by appointment. Closed January–March.)

Services and Events

Personalized private labels, gift baskets.

Directions

The winery is located in the town of Washington, southwest of Pittsburgh.

From the north, east, or west: Take I-70/79 to the Beau Street exit and go west on Route 136. Turn left on South Wade Avenue; the winery is on the right just past the next light.

From the south: Take the Laboratory exit from I-79. Go west on Route 40 (the National Pike) to the third traffic light. Turn left onto South Wade Avenue; the winery is on the right.

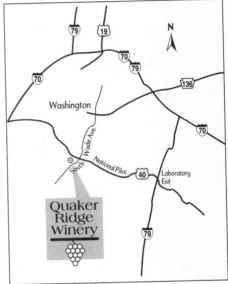

Rushland Ridge Vineyards & Winery

2665 Rushland Rd., Rushland, PA 18956
PHONE: (215) 598-0251
FAX: (215) 675-3035
E-MAIL: rrv@p3.net

LOCATION: Southeast, Philadelphia Area

WHEN ED ULLMAN WAS A TEENAGER, HE AND HIS FATHER PLANTED A FEW grapevines and began to experiment with making wine out of any fruit they could get to ferment. By the 1980s Ed and his wife, Lisa, decided they wanted to pursue growing grapes and making wine commercially. They started to look for suitable land where they could grow grapes and build a house, and in 1986 they bought a 22-acre farm in Bucks County. One acre was planted that first year, and by 1991 they were ready to open their winery. Today 3 acres are planted in a variety of French hybrid and native American grapes. Ed would like to plant up to 15 acres on the site and plans for that to happen gradually.

The Ullmans designed their house so that there would be plenty of space in the basement for making wine. The crushing pad is outside, and the grape must or juice is pumped through hoses into the tanks in the cellar. After the wines are fermented, they are cold-stabilized in tanks outside on the crushing pad. The wine is bottled in the cellar, then moved across the parking lot to the tasting room, which is located in a separate building with an equipment storage garage attached.

The winery is closed every year during January and February. We visited Rushland Ridge the first day the winery was open in March 1999. It was a cold, blustery day, and the tasting room, heated by a woodstove, was a pleasant place to taste wine. The next day, March 7, that woodstove was the cause of a fire that totally destroyed the tasting room and adjacent garage. Fortunately no one was hurt, and because the wine is stored in the wine cellar under the house, most of it survived the fire. The Ullmans reopened the winery, using the wine cellar as their salesroom, and began to rebuild the tasting room almost immediately.

All that remained of the tasting room and storage shed at Rushland Ridge Vineyards & Winery on March 7, 1999, were a blackened tank and the burnt shell of a forklift. This photo was taken while the fire trucks were still at the scene of the fire. (Photo by Jerry Forest.)

The rebuilt tasting room at Rushland Ridge Vineyards & Winery looks much the same as the one that was destroyed by fire in March 1999. On the outside, only the location of the French doors has been changed. Inside the tasting room has been completely redesigned to improve traffic flow for visitors.

We visited the winery again in late May, and substantial progress had been made on the new building. The exterior of the tasting room looks much the same as the previous one, except that double doors have been put in on the parking-lot side of the building. As a result, the interior of the tasting room has a new orientation and a different traffic flow for customers. The Ullmans hope that the new design will also allow for more flexibility in the future.

Wine List

Dry: Villard, DeChaunac, Chelois

Off-dry: Vidal, Seyval, Rosette, Red (Seyval and DeChaunac), Foch

Semisweet: Cayuga

Sweet: Ravat, Niagara, Rosé (Foch and Villard)

Best-selling Wine: Niagara

Rushland Ridge
Vineyards

BUCKS COUNTY
Villard Blanc
White Table Wine

Grown, produced and bottled for sale only in Pennsylvania by
Rushland Ridge Vineyards, Rushland PA.
Time proven methods are used to grow these wines. Our intent
is to produce wines that can be enjoyed at any meal or occasion.

The Ullmans

GOVERNMENT WARNING: (1) According to the Surgeon General women
should not drink alcoholic beverages during pregnancy because of the risk of
birth defects. (2) Consumption of alcoholic beverages impairs your ability to
drive a car or operate machinery, and may cause health problems.

Hours

Saturday, noon to 6:00 P.M.; Sunday, noon to 4:00 P.M. (Closed January–February; reopens the first weekend in March.)

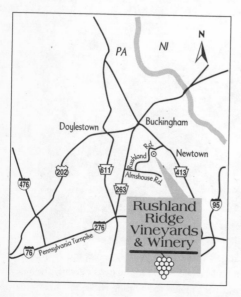

Services and Events

Picnic tables, swings for children.

Directions

The winery is located in Bucks County west of Newtown. Take Route 263 north from Philadelphia. Turn right onto Almshouse Road (Route 332). Turn left on Rushland Road, the fourth road to the left. The road makes several sharp bends before you arrive at the winery on the right.

Sand Castle Winery

755 River Rd. (Route 32), P.O. Box 177, Erwinna, PA 18920
PHONE: (800) PA2-WINE or (800) 722-9463
FAX: (610) 294-9174
E-MAIL: winesand@aol.com
WEBSITES: http://members.aol.com/winesand
www.sandcastlewinery.com

LOCATION: **Southeast, Philadelphia Area**

IN 1969 TWO BROTHERS, JOE AND PAUL MAXIAN, EMIGRATED FROM Bratislava, Slovakia, to Bucks County, Pennsylvania, and started a construction company. In just five years they were able to buy 40 acres of land along the Delaware River south of Erwinna where they planned to grow grapes and build a winery. They named the project Sand Castle to reflect the fragility of their dreams, and even today those dreams are still not totally fulfilled. The only castle visitors see at Sand Castle Winery is a drawing on the wine labels and on a diagram of the future winery building tacked to the front wall of the tasting room building. Presently, a large tent stands where the castle will be constructed.

Nevertheless, the vineyard, which has been producing grapes for more than ten years, has been expanded, and the wine production facility is in place. The winery opened in 1988 and now produces between 15,000 and 18,000 cases (35,700 to 42,800 gallons) of wine per year. Someday the tasting room will be housed in a castle on the concrete slab that is the roof of the wine cellar below. That day may come relatively soon, because the winery is increasingly cramped for space, and more vineyard acreage has come into production.

It took the Maxians almost ten years, working in their spare time, to prepare the land for a vineyard. They installed a drip irrigation system and have completely fenced the vineyard to keep out hungry deer. By 1985 they had planted 36 acres with vinifera varieties, including Riesling, Chardonnay, Pinot Noir, and Cabernet Sauvignon—one of the few wineries in Pennsylvania to grow only vinifera grapes. Joe and Paul drew on their childhood experiences working in a vineyard for their father and planted their vines close together in the European style, sixteen hundred

The winery at Sand Castle is totally underground and the temperature there is always cool, even in the heat of summer. In winter, the interior is quite cold, and Joe Maxian wears a heavy coat in the barrel area of the winery.

vines to an acre. Though this practice adds to the cost of the initial planting, the Maxians believe it helps control the vigor of the vines. The Maxians purchased another 32-acre farm in 1987 and planted about half the land with grapes.

The first part of the winery to be built was the production area. To create the necessary space, Joe and Paul blasted a 30-foot-deep hole in the rock and built a large room underground that measures 70 by 100 feet. Large tanks were installed, and the winery is prepared to produce up to 200,000 gallons, the present legal limit for a limited winery in Pennsylvania. A walkway, decorated with grape and wine-oriented murals painted by a local artist, allows visitors to look down on the wine cellar without interfering with the winemaking activities that are occurring below.

Joe, who now works full-time at the winery, describes himself as an apprentice winemaker. While he handles the day-to-day aspects of the winemaking, a winemaster is brought in from Slovakia each year to help transform the potential of Sand Castle's grapes into quality wines in a traditionally European style.

Until the new building is constructed above the wine cellar, the tasting room is housed in temporary quarters consisting of two prefabricated house trailers. Large plate-glass windows look out to the east and down the hillside toward the Delaware River.

Wine List

Dry: Johannisberg Riesling Dry, Chardonnay Private Reserve, Chardonnay Classic, Cabernet Sauvignon, Pinot Noir

Slightly Sweet: Johannisberg Riesling, Cuvée Blush

Sweet: Late Harvest Johannisberg Riesling

Best-selling Wine: Chardonnay

Hours

Monday–Saturday, 10:00 A.M. to 6:00 P.M.; Sunday, 11:00 A.M. to 6:00 P.M.

Services and Events

Three different types of tours (for which a fee is charged), including classroom education and tasting; musical events held monthly during the Spring and Summer; and two-day festivals.

Directions

The winery is located 12 miles north of New Hope on Route 32, which runs along the western shore of the Delaware River. This is a scenic approach to the winery, but for many people it may be quicker to go north from Doylestown on Route 611 to the intersection with Route 413. Take Route 413 South into the little town of Pipersville. Route 413 makes a right-hand turn at the Pipersville Tavern, but if you continue straight onto Dark Hollow Road (SR 1032), it will take you to Route 32. Dark Hollow Road winds over a one-lane bridge, past old stone farmhouses and brand new mansions for about 6 miles. When the road ends at Route 32, turn left. The winery will be on the left in 1 mile.

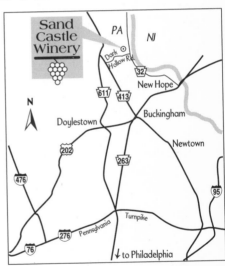

Extensions

- Old City, 149 N. 3rd St., Philadelphia, (215) 574-9463 (open Tuesday–Thursday, 4:00 to 9:00 P.M.; Friday, 1:00 to 9:00 P.M.; Saturday, noon to 9:00 P.M.; Sunday, 11:00 A.M. to 6:00 P.M.
- McCaffrey Shopping Center, Yardley, (215) 493-2648 (open daily, 3:00 to 8:00 P.M.).

🍇 Seven Valleys Vineyard & Winery

885 George's Court, Glen Rock, PA 17327
PHONE AND FAX: (717) 235-6281
WEBSITE: www.sevenvalleys.com

LOCATION: Southeast, Susquehanna Valley
(Mason-Dixon Wine Trail)

FRED HUNTER GREW UP IN CALIFORNIA AND WORKED IN THE VINEYARDS there. He always dreamed that someday he would have a vineyard and then a winery. In the 1970s he and his wife, Lynn, had two small children and were both working as psychologists in the Philadelphia area. It was not exactly California, but the Hunters began to look for a farm where they could fulfill Fred's dream of growing grapes and making wine. The farm they found was in southern York County, almost at the Pennsylvania-Maryland line.

In 1976 Lynn and Fred planted their first grapes at Seven Valleys Vineyard. Though the farm totals 85 acres, the acreage planted with grapes has never been more than 27. The Hunters think 25 acres is close to ideal, both for their particular site and because it is a size that two people can handle, using some mechanization in the vineyard. For many years, Lynn and Fred continued to live in suburban Philadelphia, where they worked at their day jobs as psychologists, and commuted to the farm for weekends and holidays. They took their vacation during harvest to bring in the grapes. They sold their grapes to other wineries and gradually developed a reputation for producing high-quality fruit.

As their sons finished high school, Lynn and Fred began to think more seriously about closing their practices in the Philadelphia area and "retiring" to York County to concentrate on growing grapes. After years of selling all of their grapes, they opened the winery in 1994. Almost immediately they opened an extension in Shrewsbury to take advantage of the traffic coming off I-83. The first extension was located on the west side of Main Street, and in 1998 the wine shop moved to its present location on the ground level of a two-hundred-year-old tavern on the east side of

Lynn Hunter and her husband Fred grew grapes for almost twenty years and sold them to other wineries before opening their own winery in 1994.

Main Street. The winery now produces about 2,500 gallons; the remainder of the grapes are sold to other wineries.

Neither Lynn nor Fred have yet retired, but their commute is shorter than it used to be. They now live full-time at the vineyard, and both are practicing psychologists in York. Their next goal is to begin to limit their practices and to move their offices out to the farm. According to Lynn, running the winery and the vineyard, living on the farm, and having their psychology practices is now lots of fun. It helps that they have found excellent people to help them with running the vineyard and winery, which gives both of them some time to do what they like best—growing grapes and making wine, while helping others.

Wine List

Dry: Seyval, Proprietor's White (Vidal, Seyval, and Cayuga), Cabernet Sauvignon

Semisweet: Vidal Blanc, Limerick (Vidal, Seyval, and Steuben), Country White (Vidal, Seyval, and Cayuga), Riesling, Country Red

(Chambourcin, Chancellor, and Vidal), Steuben Blush, Celebration (Chambourcin), Proprietor's Reserve Chambourcin

Sweet: Late Harvest Vidal

Best-selling Wines: Limerick, Celebration

Hours

Saturday and Sunday, noon to 5:00 P.M. (Other hours by appointment.)

Directions

The winery is not far from the Maryland-Pennsylvania line and I-83 south of York. Take exit 1 from I-83 for Shrewsbury. Go west on Route 851 (Forest Avenue) to the light at Main Street. Turn right on Main Street, and go 0.2 mile. Turn left onto Clearview Drive, and go 1.3 miles to Gantz Road. Turn right, and follow the road to the left. Turn right on George's Court, and go 0.3 mile to the winery.

Extension

Seven Valleys Wine Shop, 27 N. Main St. (rear), Shrewsbury, (717) 227-0257 (open Wednesday and Thursday, 11:00 A.M. to 6:00 P.M.; Friday and Saturday, 11:00 A.M. to 7:00 P.M.; Sunday, noon to 6:00 P.M.).

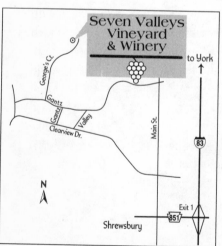

🍇 Slate Quarry Winery

460 Gower Rd., Nazareth, PA 18064
PHONE: (610) 759-0286
FAX: (610) 746-9684
E-MAIL: sidswine@aol.com

LOCATION: Southeast, Lehigh Valley
(Lehigh Valley Wine Trail)

WHILE SID AND ELLIE BUTLER HAVE RUN SLATE QUARRY WINERY FOR TEN
years, they are both grape growers at heart. In the early 1970s, when Sid
was teaching at Lehigh University and Ellie was an engineering assistant,
they decided to try a different lifestyle for themselves and their four small
children. They bought a farm near Nazareth, Pennsylvania, to begin
their "back to the land" project. They had bees and chickens, and the
idea of having their own wine from grapes they grew intrigued them.
Sid's mentor in winemaking was a math professor at Lehigh, who suggested that Sid should buy some carboys and then he would pick up
some juice from Doug Moorhead at Presque Isle Wine Cellars for Sid.
That got Sid started, and in 1971 he and Ellie planted their first grapes.

In the late 1970s no one really knew what would or would not grow
in the Lehigh Valley. Consequently, the Butlers experimented with
many different grape varietals. Today they have 13 acres planted with
both vinifera and French hybrid grapes, but the search for the right combination of grapes for their site and to make good wine continues. Sid
plans to take out the Chardonel vines because of a problem with root
borers and replace them with Florental and Kerner. Neither of these varieties is well known, but the Butlers like the light red wine that they make
from Florental. Kerner is a daughter of Riesling and seems to be easier to
grow than Riesling. It has fewer rot problems and matures earlier than its
better-known parent. Sid also likes the new variety Traminette, which, as
a wine, retains much of the aroma and flavor characteristics of its
Gewürztraminer parent. Like Kerner, Traminette has also proved to be
successful in the vineyard.

After selling all their grapes for a number of years, the Butlers decided
to open a winery in 1989, naming it for a nearby quarry. They now pro-

147

Sid Butler and his winery cat, Pinot, sit outside the entrance to the tasting room at Slate Quarry Winery.

duce some 2,000 gallons of wine each year, while continuing to sell some of their grapes to other wineries. Most of the winery's customers are from the local area.

The tasting room is at one end of the bank barn that houses the winery. A large stone fireplace beside the tasting bar is currently being used to store wine bottles for the tasting room.

Wine List

Dry: Chardonel, Chardonnay, Sauvignon Blanc, Chambourcin, Cabernet Franc, Florental

Semidry: Vidal, Quarry Stone Red (Florental), Butler's Blush (Seyval and Vidal, plus Chancellor for color), Traminette (formerly called Quarry Stone White), Kerner

Semisweet: Vignoles, Ellie's Rosé (Seyval, Vidal, and NY Muscat, plus Chancellor for color)

Sweet: Vidal Ice Wine

Sparkling: Vidal Brut, Classique Brut, Sparkling Rosé

Best-selling Wine: Ellie's Rosé

Hours

Friday–Sunday, 1:00 to 6:00 P.M. (Call for extended hours in the fall.)

Directions

From Route 22, take Route 191 north. At the blinker, take Route 946 to the left. Cross over Route 248, and go 3/4 mile to Knauss Road. Bear right onto Knauss Road, go 1/2 mile, and veer right onto Gower Road. The winery entrance is on the left in 1/4 mile. From Route 33, take the exit for Route 191 West to Nazareth. As you come into Nazareth, turn right onto High Street. When you are out in the countryside again, turn left onto Gower Road. The winery will be on the right in about 1 mile.

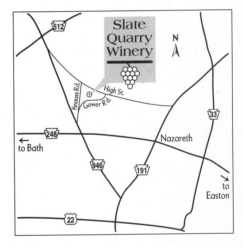

🍇 Smithbridge Cellars

159 Beaver Valley Rd., Chadds Ford, PA 19317
PHONE: (610) 558-4703
E-MAIL: wines@smithbridge.com
WEBSITE: www.smithbridge.com

LOCATION: Southeast, Philadelphia area
(Chester County Wine Trail)

THE ORIGINS OF SMITHBRIDGE CELLARS GO BACK TO 1979, WHEN JOHN F. "Trip" Stocki planted the first vines in what expanded to be a 7-acre vineyard. Trip first sold his grapes primarily to Eric Miller at Chaddsford Winery, and then decided to open his own winery in 1992. However, his first love was viticulture, not winemaking, and after five years he decided to either sell or close the winery. Meanwhile, amateur winemaker Geoff Harrington had dreamed for many years of having his own winery. In the 1980s he lived in Matamoras, Pennsylvania, where the zoning laws proved to be prohibitive. Then the Harrington family moved to Williamsport, which has a decidedly cold climate. In the interim, Geoff continued to make wine, for which he won many awards, especially from the American Wine Society amateur competitions.

In 1997 Trip contacted Geoff to see if he would be interested in buying some of his equipment. Instead, Geoff and his wife, Frances, ended up buying the entire winery. They officially opened for business on Valentine's Day in 1998. A year later the Harringtons had sold their house in Williamsport and moved closer to the winery. Trip provided some guidance with the vineyard for about six months, until he moved out of the area, and Tom Cottrell is serving as consulting winemaker.

The Harringtons have enough acreage that they could double the 7-acre vineyard in size. They plan to put in more Pinot Noir and Sauvignon Blanc, and ultimately may add more Cabernet Sauvignon, Cabernet Franc, and Merlot. Until the vineyard is producing more red wine grapes, Geoff plans to purchase local grapes and also some fruits, such as raspberries.

Geoff wants to keep Smithbridge a vinifera winery. As a result, most of the wines he produces are dry, with only the Riesling made in semidry and sweet styles. Fruit wines, including Northern Spy Apple Wine and Raspberry, provide customers with a variety of sweetness levels. The red wines are primarily Bordeaux blends. The Hearthstone Red, named for the fireplace that remains in the ruins of an old stone house by the driveway, is a blend of Cabernet Franc, Cabernet Sauvignon, and Merlot. The Reserve Red wine is a similar blend, but with more time in the barrel before the wine is released. In order to establish the red blends, the Harringtons held a barrel tasting for some customers and their employees and looked for a consensus on what people liked to drink. As often happens with wines, people liked both the varietal wines and the blended wines. In the end, Geoff and Fran had to come up with the blends to meet their goals.

The winery, named for a nearby covered bridge, is housed in a Pennsylvania bank barn that dates to the 1800s. The cow stalls are no longer in evidence, and the floor has been modified with the necessary drains that are so useful in cleaning up after making wine. The winery is equipped with stainless steel tanks of different sizes and a barrel room for aging the different wines. All that's missing is more storage space for the

Many wineries offer concerts of various types of music to entertain their customers. Here, while the Sean Fleming Band sets up to play Irish music outside the winery building at Smithbridge Cellars, visitors are bringing their wine from the tasting room to sip while listening.

finished product. The tasting room sits in one corner of the barn basement, and a picnic area is located outside.

Wine List

Dry: Hearthstone Red (Cabernet Franc, Cabernet Sauvignon, and Merlot), Reserve Red (Cabernet Sauvignon, Merlot, and Cabernet Franc, plus more time in oak), Pinot Noir, Chardonnay, Chardonnay Reserve, Sauvignon Blanc.

Semidry: Riesling

Semisweet: Riesling

Fruit Wines: Northern Spy Apple Wine, Raspberry

Hours

Saturday and Sunday, noon to 6:00 P.M. Summer hours, Wednesday–Sunday, noon to 6:00 P.M.

Services and Events

Monthly music events, harvest festival.

Directions

From the intersection of Route 1 (Baltimore Pike) and Route 202, head south on Route 202 approximately 2.2 miles. Turn right at traffic light onto Beaver Valley Road. Go approximately 1/2 mile, and turn right onto the gravel lane at the winery sign.

Extension

The Grape Vine, 224 Pine St., Williamsport, (570) 326-1111.

Stargazers Vineyard

1024 Wheatland Dr., Coatesville, PA 19320-5203
PHONE AND FAX: (610) 486-0422
E-MAIL: stargazers@kennett.net
WEBSITE: www.kennett.net/stargazers

LOCATION: Southeast, Philadelphia Area
(Chester County Wine Trail)

STARGAZERS SEEMS LIKE AN APPROPRIATELY ROMANTIC NAME FOR A VINEYARD and winery. But in the case of Stargazers Vineyard, it has another derivation. The winery, which opened in 1996, is located in Chester County not far from the stone referred to as the Stargazers' Stone, which marks the location of the observatory used by Charles Mason and Jeremiah Dixon when they were surveying the border between Pennsylvania and Maryland. Mason and Dixon were known as "the stargazers" because they used celestial navigation to correct the measurements they made on the ground. Their headquarters were in the Harlan House on the corner of Stargazers Road and Route 162. When John and Alice Weygandt started their vineyard, they used the name Stargazers because of its local association.

For fifteen years, the Weygandts grew grapes and sold the harvest to other wineries, saving only enough to make some wine for their own consumption. The original 10-acre vineyard was planted in 1979 and included vinifera varieties such as Chardonnay and Pinot Noir, as well as a number of other vinifera that have since been replaced. They started out with the rows spaced 10 feet apart and the vines 8 feet apart. Over the years, they have come to believe that vines can be planted more closely together, and their new 5-acre block of Chardonnay, Pinot Noir, Dornfelder, and Pinot Gris is planted much more closely. The new vineyard has one thousand vines per acre, whereas the older vineyard was planted with six hundred per acre. John and Alice have also used a different trellising system in the new vineyard. The older vineyard employs the Pendlebogen system, in which the canes are pruned and then bent down toward the ground and tied in place; the new vineyard utilizes the Scott

The winery building at Stargazers Vineyard was purposely built into the hill to take advantage of the cooler temperatures underground. Rainwater from the roof is collected in large cisterns built into the hill to provide some of the water needs of the winery.

Henry system, which allows the canopy to grow upward and downward from a central fruiting zone.

The winery building, like the Weygandts' home on the hill above it, is built as a passive solar building. It has no heating or cooling system, but is built into the hill to achieve a year-round moderate temperature. Rainwater is collected from the roof into cisterns that are buried in the ground beside the winery, and this water augments well water for use in the winery. A large concrete crush pad covered by a roof offers sweeping views down the vineyard on the hillside to the rolling hills of Chester County. It also provides enough room to work during harvest, with grapes coming in from the vineyard on one side or unloaded from a truck at the other end.

Inside the winery building, the back room holds bottles in stacked bins and cases of wine, while the main room houses stainless steel tanks and stainless steel barrels. The barrels have removable oak heads, which impart some oak flavor to the wine. Because the heads can be removed, various types of oak inserts can be used in the barrel, or the oak heads can be replaced with stainless ones. John uses these stainless steel barrels to add a light amount of oak to the wine as it ages.

The winery is located out in the country, and though it is a lovely drive to get there, it is not on a busy highway. As a result, the Weygandts also have an outlet in Kennett Square to take advantage of a relatively nearby population base.

Wine List

Dry: Pinot Gris, Chardonnay, Sauvignon Blanc, Cabernet Franc, Merlot

Sparkling: Pinot Noir, Riesling

Best-selling Wine: Chardonnay

Hours

Sunday, 10:00 A.M. to 6:00 P.M. (Other days by appointment.)

Directions

The winery is located in Chester County north of Unionville and south of Coatesville. From Unionville, follow Route 162 East for several miles, then turn left on Stargazers Road. After a mile or so, the road goes uphill and curves to the right. At that T, turn left onto Youngs, then make a right onto Laurel. After about 1 mile, turn right onto Wheatland and go to the top of the hill. Each of these turns is marked by a very small, hand-lettered sign, some of which are placed 10 feet or higher on a tree trunk.

Extensions

The Country Butcher, Walnut and Cypress Sts., Kennett Square, (610) 444-5980 (open Tuesday–Thursday, 9:00 A.M. to 6:00 P.M.; Friday, 9:00 A.M. to 8:00 P.M.; Saturday, 9:00 A.M. to 4:00 P.M.).

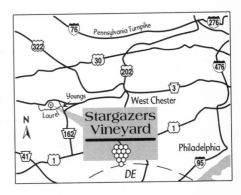

🍇 Susquehanna Valley Winery

802 Mount Zion Dr., Danville, PA 17821
PHONE: (570) 275-2364
FAX: (570) 275-5813

LOCATION: **Mountains, Central Area**

IN THE COUNTRYSIDE OF GERMANY OR SWITZERLAND, THE FARMHOUSE AND the barn often are one structure. Sometimes the barn is at one end of the building; other times it is on the ground-floor level and the family lives upstairs. Susquehanna Valley Winery near Danville is reminiscent of one of these farmhouses, with the winery in the section of the building originally planned as the horse barn and the Latranyi family living upstairs. The tasting room is also on the lower level. The house is of stucco and beam construction, with lace curtains in the windows. The entire effect is that one has been transported to some part of southern Germany.

In fact, Nick and Hildegarde Latranyi bought the 203-acre farm on the hills above the Susquehanna River because the location reminded them of the Rhine River Valley. Nick came to the United States in 1958 from Hungary, where his father grew about 2 acres of grapes and made some wine in a cooperative-type winery; Hildegarde came from a similar background in southern Germany. Hildegarde wanted to grow some grapes and make jams and jellies; she also wanted to raise their two sons somewhere other than New Jersey, where Nick was working for a major drug company. While Nick worked in New Jersey and commuted to the farm on weekends (he describes himself as "the weekend guest"), Hildegarde and their sons, Mark and Eric, built their house using wooden beams harvested from their woods. It was designed by Hildegarde to be similar to the houses she knew in Germany. As in Germany, the barn was to be under one end of the house.

One major problem was a source of water. Although the property overlooks the Susquehanna River, it is high on top of a hill. The Latranyis dug seven wells in various locations on the farm before they found a source for a small amount of water. They also use catch basins to retain rainwater in a field above the house.

The vineyard of 3 acres was planted more than fifteen years ago with native American and hybrid grapes including Niagara, Concord, Delaware, Elvira, Catawba, Moore's Diamond, Aurore, and Baco Noir. The Latranyis don't use herbicides and are trying to grow all their grapes organically. Their major problem, however, is birds. The family has a flock of peacocks, which at one time numbered thirty-five, and the vineyard has also been discovered by turkeys, grouse, starlings, and other birds that like to eat fresh, sweet grapes. So far the Latranyis have not used netting but try to scare the birds away by other methods. The fruiting zone of the grapes was quite low in the original vineyard, and the trellis is currently being redone and the vines retrained so that the grapes will not be as low to the ground.

The Latranyis' original purpose of growing grapes was to provide fruit for Hildegarde's jams and jellies. When they discovered they had too

The Latranyi family designed a European-style farm winery when they built their home and winery at Susquehanna Valley Winery. The family lives upstairs; the tasting room and winery are on the ground floor.

many grapes for jelly, they began to make wine. They converted the barn section of the house to a winery, which now produces between 400 and 2,000 gallons of wine per year. In 1998 they purchased 1,300 gallons of juice to supplement their own grapes. Hildegarde was originally the winemaker for the family. Now, Mark and Eric, who both work other jobs during the week, return home to help with the winemaking on weekends.

People in the local area prefer sweet wines, and as they are the primary market for the winery, those are the wines that the Latranyis make. Even the wines listed as dry have some sweetness to them.

The tasting room is on the ground-floor level of the house. Part of the room is the family rec room, with a bar area that serves as the tasting room. The winery carries some gift items and wine accessories.

Wine List

Dry: Vidal Blanc, Dry Duet (Baco Noir and Steuben)

Semidry: Symphony (white hybrid and native American grapes), Baco Noir

Sweet: Sweet Niagara, Sweet Concord, Melody

Sweet Spiced Wines: Summer Sonata (white wine blend plus spices to use as a Sangria or wine cooler), Glühwein (red wine blend plus spices to use as a hot mulled wine)

Best-selling Wine: Glühwein

Hours

Wednesday–Sunday, 1:00 to 6:00 P.M.

Services and Events

Special labels for events such as weddings.

Directions

Susquehanna Valley Winery is located south of Route 11 and a few miles east of Danville.

From the east: Take I-80 to exit 34 at Buckhorn; turn south on Route 11 toward Danville. Look for the Jack Metzger Ford and Volkswagen dealership on the right; turn left there onto Ridge Drive (there is a winery sign). Go about 1 mile to the next crossroad, and turn right on Mount Zion Drive. Follow the signs for another mile or so to the winery.

From the west: Take I-80 to exit 33. Follow Route 54 South into Danville. Turn left on Route 11 toward Bloomsburg, and go to the Jack Metzger dealership east of Danville. Turn right on Ridge Drive, and follow the directions above.

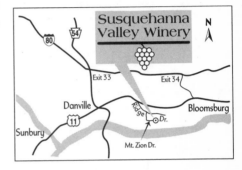

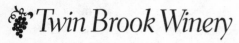 *Twin Brook Winery*

5697 Strasburg Rd., Gap, PA 17527
PHONE: (717) 442-4915

LOCATION: **Southeast, Susquehanna Valley**
(Chester County Wine Trail)

MANY PENNSYLVANIA WINERIES ARE LOCATED IN BARNS OF ONE TYPE OR another, but few are as attractive to the consumer as the Twin Brook Winery. The property has a 250-year history, as it was part of a land grant made to the Sadsbury Friends Meeting in 1741, possibly by the brother of William Penn. The stone manor house dates back to the eighteenth century, and the frame bank barn, most recently used as a dairy operation, was built in the nineteenth century.

The barn required major renovation to turn it into a winery. The interior was gutted, new walls were installed, and a concrete floor was poured. Two decks were added outside the winery, and there are picnic tables for anyone wanting to bring a lunch along. Not far from the parking lot is a large gazebo on the edge of the vineyards that can be used for picnicking. It also serves as the stage for winery concerts held on summer weekends. From the gazebo, the vineyards slope down the hill toward the juncture of the two brooks that give the winery its name. If harvest is imminent, the vines will be covered with netting to deter migratory birds from eating the grapes before they can be picked to make wine.

The vineyards were planted in 1985, and today more than 30 acres are producing. Seven acres are planted with French hybrid grapes, and the remaining 23 are planted with vinifera grapes, including Chardonnay, Pinot Gris, Cabernet Sauvignon, Cabernet Franc, and a small amount of Merlot. The grapes produced are more than enough to supply the needs of the winery, and Twin Brook sells both fresh fruit and juice during harvest to other wineries looking for a good supply of quality grapes.

The winery was founded by Richard and Cheryl Caplan. Both were trained as lawyers, but today only Richard is a practicing attorney. He serves as the president of the winery, and Cheryl is the vineyard manager, winemaker, chief marketer, and full-time administrator. Since the winery opened in 1990, Cheryl has been on-site, supervising all aspects of the vineyard and winery operations, planning events, and handling the marketing. Currently the winery produces between 8,000 and 10,000 gallons, in addition to selling fresh fruit and grape juice.

The tasting room was established on the upper level of the restored bank barn and features a nineteenth-century carved oak bar that was salvaged from an old hotel in New Holland, Pennsylvania, and stained-glass windows from a demolished church. A second level of the tasting area is reached by a handmade spiral staircase whose central support column was made from a walnut tree trunk cut from a tree on the property. Glass windows allow visitors to look down on the main winemaking and tank storage area of the winery on the lower floor, while windows on the other side of the wide hall open on the room where the wine is bottled.

Birds can be a major problem for grape growers when the grapes become sweet and juicy. The solution at Twin Brook Winery is to apply netting to cover all the vines after the grapes begin to ripen and their color turns from green to purple. The netting is removed, carefully, before the grapes are harvested, rerolled, and stored for use the following season.

Wine List

Dry: Chardonnay, Pinot Gris, Merlot, Cabernet Franc, Cabernet Sauvignon, Chancellor

Semidry: Cayuga, Vidal Blanc, Icebreaker Blush, Consiglieri, Octorara Rosé

Semisweet: Vignoles, Octorara Red, Blossom Blush

Sweet: Clocktower White, Springhouse White, Strasburger Red, Spice Wine

Best-selling Wine: Icebreaker Blush (Cayuga and Vidal, with some Foch for color)

Hours

January 1–March 31, Tuesday–Sunday, noon to 5:00 P.M.; April 1–December 31, Monday–Saturday, 10:00 A.M. to 6:00 P.M.; Sunday, noon to 5:00 P.M.

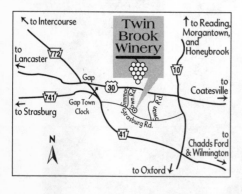

Directions

The winery is located on the Lancaster–Chester County line approximately 18 miles east of Lancaster and about 3 miles from Route 30.

From Philadelphia: Take 202 South to Route 30 West. Cross Route 10, and continue 2.1 miles to Swan Road. Turn left on Swan Road, then right on Strasburg Road. The winery will be on the right.

From Lancaster: Take Route 30 East approximately 18 miles; turn right on Swan Road, then right on Strasburg Road.

Extension

Basketville Store, 3361 Lincoln Hwy. East, Paradise, (717) 442-9379 (open seven days a week; hours may vary with the season).

🍇 Vynecrest Winery

172 Arrowhead Lane, Breinigsville, PA 18031
PHONE: (800) 361-0725, (610) 398-7525
FAX: (610) 398-7530
E-MAIL: landisjg@ptd.net
WEBSITE: vynecrest.com

LOCATION: Southeast, Lehigh Valley
(Lehigh Valley Wine Trail)

VYNECREST WINERY CELEBRATED TWO MAJOR ANNIVERSARIES IN 1999: IT was twenty-five years since John and Jan Landis planted their first vineyard, and ten years since they opened the winery. The Landises marked these major milestones by completely renovating the turn-of-the-century bank barn that houses the winery. Previously, both the winemaking facility and the tasting room had been in the bottom part of the barn, and the second floor was used for storage. As the winery grew, it became apparent that they needed both a bigger tasting room and more space for wine production.

In 1998, John retired from his position at Air Products Company, where, as an engineer, he had designed innovations for waste treatment plants. When he started working full-time at the winery, he had time to tackle the renovation project. He hired two local craftsmen to help him, and in six months they completely renovated the second floor of the barn to include a bottling room with case storage, offices, restroom facilities, and a spacious tasting room with large windows facing to the south. The entire area is open to the ceiling, which was insulated, covered with old but newly painted garage door panels, and fitted with ceiling fans. The original post-and-beam construction of the barn and even the hayloft ladders were left exposed as walls were created to divide the area into the appropriate spaces. The result is a modern tasting room filled with light from the large southerly windows and plenty of space for the tasting bar and a gift shop area, while the ambience of the old barn remains intact.

The winery is expanding in other ways as well. While John is currently making about 2,000 gallons of wine each year, he has the space to produce as much as 5,000 gallons. The farm has a total of 33 acres, with 6 acres of vineyard currently producing. The Landises feel strongly about

The second floor of the barn at Vynecrest Winery was renovated into offices and an attractive new tasting room after John Landis retired from his "day job" and became full time at the winery.

growing all the grapes they use for wine so that their wines are all "estate bottled," and as a result, they recently planted 2 more acres with varieties such as Pinot Blanc, Cabernet Franc, and Viognier. There is enough acreage available that the vineyard could grow to 26 acres.

How big both the vineyard and the winery become depends to a degree on whether either of the Landises' two sons decide to become more involved in the winery. For now, John would like to keep the winery at a size where he and Jan can handle all aspects of growing the grapes, making the wine, and running the tasting room themselves. John is enjoying his new career as full-time winemaker, barn renovator, and winery owner.

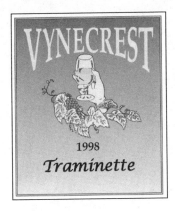

Wine List

Dry: Seyval, Traminette, Chambourcin, Baco Noir

Semisweet: Vidal, Arrowhead White (Traminette, Gewürztraminer, and Vidal), Arrowhead Red (Lemberger, Baco Noir, and Cayuga)

Sweet: Autumn Gold (Cayuga and Vidal, late harvest style)

Best-selling Wine: Arrowhead White

Hours

Thursday–Sunday, 1:00 to 6:00 P.M.

Services and Events

Personalized labels.

Directions

The winery is approximately 7 miles west of Allentown. Take Route 78/22 west to exit 1A, Route 100 South. At the second traffic light on Route 100, turn right onto Schantz Road. After 1.6 miles, turn right onto Arrowhead Lane. The winery is on the left in ¹/2 mile.

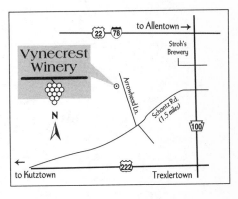

West Hanover Winery

7646 Jonestown Rd., Harrisburg, PA 17112
PHONE: (717) 652-3711, (800) 532-7994
FAX: (717) 651-0409

LOCATION: **Southeast, Susquehanna Valley**

IF YOU VISIT ANY OF THE WINE-GROWING AREAS OF GERMANY, YOU'LL FIND that many suburban homes actually include a small winery. The family lives in the house, the backyard has a concrete crushing pad and a garage or small barn for equipment, and the family winery is in the basement. West Hanover Winery is just such a winery, except that it is east of Harrisburg, Pennsylvania, and not in the Rheingau. Only the small parking lot in front of the house and a wooden sign announcing the presence of Kline's Vineyard and the West Hanover Winery indicate that the house is any different from other homes along the street.

George Kline describes his winery as "a hobby that got out of hand." For thirty-eight years he worked as a meat cutter but also started making wine at home. He planted a few vines, and then in 1990 he began to plant grapes on land that belonged to his mother. He purchased 2 acres next to his parents' house and designed a home that would be a typical suburban house, but with room for a winery in the daylight basement beneath. George retired from the meat business and began his new career as a winemaker. Late in 1997 he opened the winery in his basement.

He is now producing between 600 and 1,000 gallons of wine per year in nineteen different varieties. His market is primarily local people who like their wine to be at least a bit sweet, if not very sweet. As a result, all of his wines are finished with some residual sugar, even those that are indicated as dry on his wine list.

George has planted 2,300 vines on his land and behind his parents' house, which he now owns. Though he does not have much more acreage to plant, he is encouraging a friend to plant as much as 5 acres of vines in the next year or two.

The vineyard, known as Kline's Vineyard, is planted mostly with native American varieties such as Niagara, Concord, and Catawba, as well as some hybrids, including Baco Noir, Cayuga, and Villard. The vines are planted close together, 3 to 4¹/2 feet apart, with the rows tightly spaced as well. This allows more vines to be planted on an acre of land and decreases the vigor of each individual vine. George also grows his own blueberries and red and black raspberries. The vineyard is surrounded by many trees, and as the grapes ripen, they become very attractive to the local bird population. Consequently, as soon as the grapes start to color, George applies bird netting to the entire vineyard.

Located in the basement of George's house, the winery is small but has room to grow and can potentially produce as much as 5,000 gallons. George plans to reduce the number of wines he is making, possibly by blending some varieties, but also guided by what his customers seem to prefer. The tasting room is pine paneled and features a pine tasting bar.

George Kline, owner of West Hanover Winery, examines some of his Niagara vines during the winter of 1999.

Wine List

Semidry: Cayuga, Catawba, Steuben, Concord Dry, Baco Noir

Semisweet: Niagara, Villard Blanc, Aurore, Valiant, Concord, Baco Noir, King of the North, Red Raspberry, Apple

Sweet: Sour Cherry, Blueberry, Pear

Sparkling: Apple-Concord

Best-selling Wine: Red Raspberry

Hours

Tuesday–Thursday, noon to 6:30 P.M.; Friday, Noon to 8:00 P.M.; Saturday, noon to 5:00 P.M.

Services and Events

Special labels for weddings and other events.

Directions

West Hanover Winery is located in Dauphin County, east of Harrisburg and 7 miles north of Hershey. From the intersection of Route I-81 and Route 39, go south on Route 39. Turn right on Jonestown Road; the winery is on the right in 0.9 of a mile.

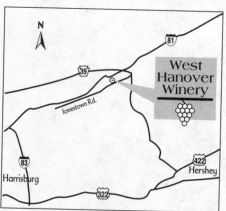

🍇 *Windgate Vineyards*

Hemlock Acres Rd., R.D. 1
Box 213, Smicksburg, PA 16256
PHONE: (814) 257-8797
FAX: (814) 257-8616

LOCATION: **Mountains, Northwest Area**

IN 1972 DAN AND LILLIAN ENERSON BOUGHT A 110-ACRE FARM OUTSIDE Smicksburg to be a weekend place where they could relax and someday retire. The first part of that goal didn't last long. Dan planted a vineyard in 1973, only to have every vine eaten by the local deer population. The next year he put up an 8-foot deer fence and replanted the vineyard. At that time, there were few wineries in Pennsylvania, as the Limited Winery Act had only been passed in 1968. There were no vineyards anywhere near the Enersons, so Dan turned to Philip Wagner in Maryland for advice on what to plant. His initial planting of five thousand vines came from Philip's nursery and included Aurore, Seyval, Foch, and DeChaunac, all of which have done well on his site. He tried other varietals, including Cascade and Chancellor, which also did well. Ravat and Léon Millot, on the other hand, did not work in his particular location.

For many years, the Enersons made homemade wine and sold the bulk of their grapes. When Dan, a cardiovascular surgeon, retired in 1987, the Enersons opened the winery. There hasn't been much relaxation since; as Dan says, "This is more work than I ever thought!" Dan still has not moved out to the winery from suburban Pittsburgh, choosing instead to commute the 60 miles each way every day.

The vineyard's production has not kept pace with the expansion of the winery, even though there are now 15 acres planted. This is partly because the initial plantings of grapes are getting old and not producing as well as in the past. Consequently, Dan is participating in a study with Penn State to try to determine the cause and ultimate solution to vineyard decline as the vines get to be more than twenty years old. And he has been planting new vines, most of which are Chambourcin.

Dan Enerson proudly displays one of the award-winning wines at Windgate Vineyards.

How does a vineyard survive in central Pennsylvania? The answer lies partly in planting varieties that will do well in a cold climate and partly in the site itself. The vineyard at Windgate is on a plateau more than 500 feet above the Mahoning Valley. The sandy soils provide good drainage, and the slope and southern exposure result in good air circulation and drainage. The temperature patterns for the farm match those of Wurzburg, Germany, although there are both more rainfall and more humidity in Smicksburg than in Wurzburg. Winter temperatures can get quite cold, although most winters do not see lows colder than about -5 degrees F.

Over the years, the winery has grown and prospered. It now produces about 8,000 gallons each year, and Dan expects that to increase.

Windgate Vineyards is in Amish country, which is something of a tourist attraction for people from Pittsburgh, approximately 70 miles away. The winery is also close to the university town of Indiana and to Punxsutawney, the center of much hoopla on Groundhog's Day. Every year the winery releases its most popular wine, Eye of the Shadow, on Groundhog's Day, February 2, with an appropriate label showing a groundhog and its shadow.

There are a large number of antique tractor collectors in the area, and each fall the winery sponsors a local tractor show that attracts many people to the winery to look at antique tractors—and try the local wine. Live music events have also proved to be popular.

Wine List

Dry: Chardonnay, Seyval Blanc, DeChaunac, Eye of the Buck (DeChaunac, Foch, Chancellor, and Cabernet Franc), Maréchal Foch

Semidry: Amish Country White (Vidal and Seyval), Aurore, Vidal Blanc, Spring Rosé (Cascade and Seyval), Amish Blush (Seyval, Vidal, Aurore, and Chancellor), Rhapsody (in Blue—bottle, that is; Vignoles)

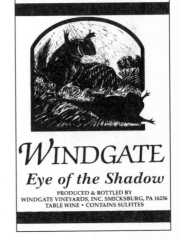

Semisweet: Eye of the Shadow (Chambourcin and Seyval)

Sweet: Amish Country Red (Foch, DeChaunac, Chancellor, Cabernet Franc, and Seyval)

Fruit Wines: Windgate Apple, Windgate Spiced Apple

Sparkling: Champagne (Chardonnay and Seyval), Sparkling Riesling

Best-selling Wines: Eye of the Shadow, Amish Country White

Hours

Daily (except holidays), noon to 5:00 P.M.

Services and Events

Picnic tables, gift shop, gift baskets, personalized labels, music and barbeque festival in June, tractor show in September.

Directions

From Pittsburgh: Take Rt. 28 north to Kittanning and Route 85. Go east on Route 85 for 12 miles to Route 839, and turn left. Where the sign says "Smicksburg—3 miles," turn right, and go 3 miles to Route 954. Follow through Smicksburg, and in 3 miles, turn left onto Hemlock Acres Road. The winery is on the right in 2 miles.

From I-80 and DuBois: Take Route 119 south to Route 210, and turn right. At the intersection with Route 954 and 210, go straight onto Route

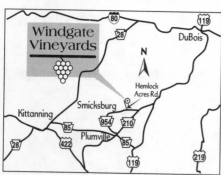

954 (Route 210 turns left). Go 2 miles, and turn right onto Hemlock Acres Road. The winery is on the right in 2 miles.

Extension

Indiana Mall, Indiana, (724) 463-8600 (open Monday–Saturday, 10:00 A.M. to 9:00 P.M.; Sunday, 11:00 A.M. to 5:00 P.M.).

🍇 *The Winery at Wilcox*

Box 39, Mefferts Run Rd., Wilcox, PA 15870
PHONE AND FAX: (814) 929-5598
E-MAIL: carolwaw@penn.com
WEBSITE: www.users.penn.com/~carolwaw/

LOCATION: **Mountains, Northwest Area**

WHEN MIKE AND CAROL WILLIAMS DECIDED TO OPEN A WINERY, THEY took advantage of the space they had available—an old goat barn next to their house, a facility Mike had used as a deer-processing plant for local hunters. Mike built a small tasting room that would accommodate about five people at the tasting bar, and the Williamses opened the winery in 1994 with 1,100 gallons of wine to sell. Over the next five years, the winery was expanded four times and increased production to 20,000 gallons.

A rural location halfway between DuBois and Bradford in northwestern Pennsylvania may not seem to be the best place to open a winery, which depends on having many visitors stop and purchase the wines. Nevertheless, Mike and Carol, whose goal was to make reasonably priced wine that the local working people would like to drink, appear to have known what they were doing. Although the winery is on a country road, the road leads to a popular camping, hunting, and fishing area. During the winery's first year, thirty-thousand people stopped in to taste the wine, and in 1998 the Williamses sold more than 12,000 gallons at the winery facility alone. Mike and Carol also opened two extensions in shopping malls in Bradford and DuBois.

The Williamses have named some of their wines for nearby landmarks. Their most popular wine, Clarion River Red, is named for the Clarion River, which runs through Wilcox; Mefferts Run Red takes its name from the road the winery is located on; East Branch Sunset is named for the East Branch of the Clarion River and the East Branch Dam, just down the road; Kinzua is a local area name and the inspiration for the blend of Vignoles and Chancellor called Kinzua Kiss; and Rasse-

Mike Williams, winemaker and co-owner of The Winery at Wilcox, has expanded his winery facility four times in five years to accommodate the rapid growth of the winery. Here he stands in front of the bottling line that can fill approximately 30 bottles per minute.

las Rosé is named for the road from Wilcox to Instanter. Other names were inspired by family or friends: Brittany's Blush is named for a grand-daughter of the Williamses; Fred's Red is made from Fredonia grapes and is named for Fred Habicht, Sr., a next-door neighbor, and his son, Fred, Jr., both strong supporters of the winery.

The Winery at Wilcox has grown quickly, and Mike anticipates that it will continue to grow. He and Carol plan to add two new retail loca-tions, one in State College and one in Cranberry. As the demand for their wine increases, so will the size of the winery. The only limitation that Mike foresees is the problem of purchasing enough grapes. Most of the grapes come from North East in Erie County; the rest come from the southeastern part of the state. In 1997, when supplies of grapes were lim-ited because of a small harvest, Mike expanded the product line to include sparkling wine made from different fruits. He first added a sparkling wine made from blueberries, called Blueberry Mist, and now also sells Peach Mist, Strawberry Mist, and Cherry Mist. In 1999 Peach Mist won the Governor's Cup at the Pennsylvania Wine Competition.

The tasting room has also been expanded since the winery first opened. The original countertop with its multiple wine labels, sealed with polyurethane, stands in a corner of the new tasting area, which can handle many more than five people. Shelves hold various gift items for purchase, and a room behind the tasting area allows the staff to create gift baskets quickly while customers wait.

Wine List

Dry: Chardonnay, Seyval Blanc, Léon Millot, Chambourcin, Cabernet Franc

Semidry: Brittany's Blush (Catawba with a red hybrid for color), Mefferts Run Red (Foch), Autumn Leaves (Concord, DeChaunac, and Baco Noir)

Semisweet: Riesling, Vidal Blanc, East Branch Sunset (Chancellor and Vidal), Hunter Red (Concord), Kinzua Kiss (Vignoles and Chancellor), Rasselas Rosé (Concord and Catawba), Vignoles, Bear-ly Blush (Steuben), Wedding White (Catawba)

Sweet: Bob White (field blend of Diamond, Chardonnay, Seyval, and Delaware), Angelique (Riesling), Fred's Red (Fredonia), Niagara, Clarion River Red (Concord, Niagara, and Baco Noir), Spiced Apple

Sparkling: Celebration (Catawba, Brut-style), Blueberry Mist, Peach Mist, Strawberry Mist, Cherry Mist

Best-selling Wines: Clarion River Red, Wedding White

Hours

January, daily, noon to 6:00 P.M.; February–December, daily, 10:00 A.M. to 6:00 P.M.

Services and Events

Gift baskets, special labels.

Directions

Take I-80 to exit 16. Go north on Route 219 toward Bradford. 1.5 miles north of Johnsonburg, turn right on Mefferts Run Road. The winery is on the left in 1.9 miles.

Extensions

- Bradford Wine Shop, 83 Main St., Bradford, (814) 362-1981 (open Monday–Thursday and Saturday, 10:00 A.M. to 6:00 P.M.; Friday, 10:00 A.M. to 8:00 P.M.; Sunday, noon to 5:00 P.M.).
- DuBois Wine Shop, Route 255 & Shaffer Rd., DuBois, (814) 375-6885 (open Monday–Saturday, 10:00 A.M. to 9:00 P.M.; Sunday, noon to 5:00 P.M.).
- Other extensions are planned at Cranberry Mall, in Franklin, and Nittany Mall, in State College.

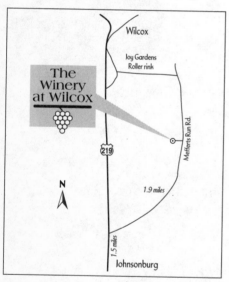

FUTURE PENNSYLVANIA WINERIES

OPENING A WINERY IS A PROCESS THAT TAKES QUITE A LONG TIME. IT'S NOT just a matter of having a location, a name, making enough wine, and opening the doors to the public; there are many legal requirements on local, state, and federal levels that must be met before a winery can officially be in business. In the course of preparing this guide to Pennsylvania wineries, we talked with a number of people who were interested in opening a winery. Some of them probably will never open to the public; others need only a final approval from the Pennsylvania Liquor Control Board or the Bureau of Alcohol, Tobacco and Firearms.

The following is a list of wineries that will likely open, along with each winery's address, owner, and the projected opening date. For the latest information on these wineries, check the website for this book (www.vitis-ir.com/pawine); watch the listings in the *Pennsylvania Wine Traveler*, the newspaper published by the Pennsylvania Wine Association and available in all State Stores; or call the telephone numbers provided to determine whether a new winery has actually opened.

Wineries now open

Bashore & Stoudt Country Winery

5784 Old Route 22, P.O. Box 167, Shartlesville, PA 19554
David Bashore and Bob Stoudt, (610) 488-9466
Hours: Thursday–Sunday, 11:00 A.M. to 6:00 P.M.

Possible new wineries

Benigna's Creek Vineyard & Winery (summer 2000)

R.D. 1, Box 166, Klingerstown, PA 17941
Rick Masser, (570) 425-2469
Lisa King, Marketing, (717) 244-1279

La Casa Narcisi (early 2000)

Route 910, Gibsonia, PA 15041
Sarah and Dennis Narcisi

Millcreek Winery (spring 2000)

10 First St., Fredonia, PA 16124
Gary A. Rhodes, (724) 475-3185

Plum Run Winery (fall 1999)

11 Necessary St., Beallsville, PA 15313
Joe Skocik, (724) 632-3147

Shade Mountain Winery (fall 1999)

R.D. 2, Box 24, Middleburg, PA 17842
(Winery located 2 miles north of Middleburg on Route 104)
Carl and Carolyn Zimmerman

Stone Villa Wine Cellars (summer 2000)

R.D. 1, Box 223A, Clay Pike Rd., Acme, PA 15610
Randall L. Paul, (724) 547-5401

Swan Valley Winery

5067 Homestead Dr., Coopersburg, PA 18036
Edward L. Ulrich

☙ INDEX